The Effective Use of Sponsorship

Marketing in Action Series

Series Editor: Norman Hart

In producing this series, the advice and assistance has been sought of a prestigious editorial panel representing the principal professional bodies, trade associations and business schools.

The Series Editor for the Marketing in Action books is Norman Hart who is a writer of some ten books himself. He currently runs his own marketing consultancy, and is also an international lecturer at marketing and other such conferences as well as the leading business schools.

The Effective Use of Sponsorship

David Wragg

Series Editor: Norman Hart

KOGAN PAGE

First published in 1994

Apart from any fair dealing for the purposes of research or private study, or criticism or review, as permitted under the Copyright, Designs and Patents Act, 1988, this publication may only be reproduced, stored or transmitted, in any form or by any means, with the prior permission in writing of the publishers, or in the case of reprographic reproduction in accordance with the terms of licences issued by the Copyright Licensing Agency. Enquires concerning reproduction outside those terms should be sent to the publishers at the undermentioned address:

Kogan Page Limited
120 Pentonville Road
London N1 9JN

© David Wragg, 1994

British Library Cataloguing in Publication Data

A CIP record for this book is available from the British Library.

ISBN 0 7494 1126 0

Typeset by DP Photosetting, Aylesbury, Bucks
Printed and bound in Great Britain by Biddles Ltd, Guildford and King's Lynn

Contents

Introduction

Sponsorship has become an important aspect of the marketing and public relations programmes of most companies today. The sponsorship marketplace has become wider and more complicated with the advent of new opportunities and with the need to think and plan internationally. There is also the growing importance of social or community sponsorships, which are sometimes allied to a company's charitable donations, forming part of the overall 'corporate giving'.

Whether directly involved or not, everyone in marketing or public relations has to appreciate the opportunities presented by these activities, the pitfalls to be avoided, and the steps that are essential to success. To achieve success, it is necessary to negotiate effectively and cooperate with the organisers of sponsored events. You must also guide colleagues in other departments and other disciplines convincing them that the chosen course of action is the right one.

Despite its long history, sponsorship is still misunderstood by organisers and by those working for sponsoring companies. This book brings the reader up-to-date with developments in sponsorship and charitable donations. It highlights the snares to be avoided and the opportunities to be grasped so that the maximum benefit can be gained from these high profile and sensitive activities.

David W Wragg
April 1994

Chapter 1

Sponsorship and Charitable Donations Today

Combining the management of both sponsorship and charitable donations in a single volume might appear strange at first. Further consideration soon shows that these two activities are at the opposite ends of a wide spectrum involving businesses providing funds to outsiders. The big difference is that sponsorship should always be a business transaction, whereas little or nothing is sought in return for most charitable donations. Over the years, a large and growing area of overlap has arisen between sponsorship and charitable donations as sponsors have embraced such activities as 'community sponsorship' or 'social sponsorship'.

Sponsorship should always be a business transaction.

Although total expenditure on sponsorship is much less than on advertising, the extent of these activities is much wider than is commonly supposed. Expenditure on sponsorship in the UK alone is estimated to be in excess of £500 million annually. This figure does not include the many additional items of expenditure, including advertising, which may be necessary to support a major sponsorship programme. Precise figures for expenditure on sponsorship are difficult to obtain. This is partly because of the fragmented nature of sponsorship, and because the value of certain areas of sponsorship, including motor sport, are a well-guarded secret.

The annual value of business donations to charity amounts to almost £200 million a year. Although these sums are lower than for sponsorship, it is believed that 99 per cent of all British companies provide charitable donations. British charities have an annual income, including trading, of £16 billion, although this is down from the peak of £18 billion achieved in 1991. These figures do not include the cost of staff seconded by businesses, or the provision by the business community of facilities or services to charities either free of charge or at a reduced rate.

Who's responsible for sponsorship?

Marketing involvement with these activities will vary. Marketing will usually have responsibility for sponsorship, but it can belong to public relations, and both functions need to be involved if full value is to be obtained. Charitable donations might be handled by marketing, or by public relations if it has a wider corporate or community affairs function. Often the company secretary or the personnel director will have ownership of this activity.

In contrast to many other aspects of marketing, the chairman or the chief executive of your company is likely to take a close interest in both sponsorship and charitable donations.

It might appear that sponsorship is no more high profile than your latest advertising campaign, but there is a more personal aspect to sponsorship that will involve others in decision making. A chairman or chief executive can shrug off a consumer advertising campaign, especially if the target audience is not perceived as a peer group. However, the presence of directors and senior management and their guests at sponsored events will create a wider involvement and a degree of interest extending far beyond the marketing department.

Another element that is well known to many sponsorship and charities' coordinators is the 'chairman's wife syndrome'. Many directors are accompanied by their spouses at a sponsored or charitable event and are susceptible to their views. The fact that these opinions may not be based on an understanding of your objectives, or even of the activity or event itself, is irrelevant.

Sponsorship and marketing.

You cannot ignore sponsorship as an element in the marketing mix. There are many reasons why companies, and indeed other organisations, sponsor. Sponsorship can raise the profile, another is to ensure good media coverage. If you have a bank of mature products that is selling steadily but with little product innovation, the newspapers will not be writing about your brand or product. Advertising will help, but if you want to benefit from editorial mentions, a good sponsorship programme could be one way to achieve this.

The term 'sponsorship' is often misused. It has passed into the language and is used carelessly, just as some people say 'marketing' when they really mean 'sales'. You will find people 'sponsoring' when they are really doing something else, mounting a corporate hospitality exercise for example.

Most people understand the term 'charitable donation', but there is a great deal that falls in between this and sponsorship.

DEFINITIONS

Jargon should be avoided whenever possible in business, but it is important to use the correct terminology, understand the differences and be consistent. One cannot expect colleagues in other disciplines to be precise about their activities if the professionals do not set an example. The differences are important, and are greater than simply splitting hairs.

If a regional manager is enthusiastic about a sponsorship proposition, you should both know that the difference between sponsorship and corporate hospitality can be substantial in both benefits and cost. So let us look first at definitions of those terms most commonly in use.

Sponsorship

Sponsorship can be defined as the support of an activity or an event from which the sponsor expects to derive a tangible benefit. The support must add substantially to the economics of the activity. On its own, a block booking of seats for a performance of 'Hamlet' or to watch a rugby international is not sponsorship.

At one time, sponsorship might have been defined as supporting an event that would not be commercially viable and self-financing without the sponsorship. Today, this is no longer always true. Many events would indeed fail without the support of a sponsor, but some could still go ahead if on a less lavish scale.

Sponsors must have definite objectives. These can include raising the organisation's profile or that of its brands or products. Sponsorship can also influence potential customers, investors, or prominent people in the community.

Essential to any worthwhile sponsorship is an agreement between the organisers and the sponsor. In exchange for accepted levels of financial support, the organisers agree to fulfil certain criteria. Commercial concerns sponsor to meet definite objectives, not simply for the sake of it.

Patronage

Even today, many sponsors are really indulging in patronage. This is the old-fashioned term for sponsorship, but it can also describe a more altruistic and less commercial form of sponsorship. When the aristocracy sponsored struggling artists or composers, success could not be guaranteed and the arrangement lacked the definite benefits expected from simple sponsorship. Sometimes the patron expected to benefit from the success of the protégé, if only from reflected glory, but other reasons were also apparent.

If your company is asked to sponsor a theatre or the performing arts in return for listing your company's name as one of the sponsors in the foyer, the request is really for patronage. There is nothing wrong in this as long as it is recognised as such. And whatever the label in the foyer might say, you and your colleagues do not proclaim it to be a sponsorship.

Corporate hospitality or entertainment

Many sponsors confuse corporate hospitality or entertainment with sponsorship, and although sponsorship will often include corporate hospitality, the two are not synonymous.

Hosting guests at a sporting or artistic occasion is an example of corporate hospitality, but it does not necessarily entail being a sponsor. Childs, the private bank, used to sponsor horse racing in a modest way, sponsoring a race at Cheltenham and entertaining wealthy clients on the day. Eventually the bankers realised that client entertainment could still continue without sponsoring the race, saving £25,000 in the process.

Even without full-blown sponsorship, corporate hospitality can still include such pleasant features as pre-performance or pre-match drinks or a meal, and refreshments at the interval or at half-time. If this is all your company needs, why spend more pretending that it is a sponsor?

Smaller companies or those with tight budgets can enjoy many of the benefits of sponsorship at an affordable cost, simply by confining themselves to corporate hospitality.

Product Promotion

Enabling a competitor in a sporting event to use your company's products is not sponsorship, but product promotion. It doesn't matter whether it is a tennis racket at Wimbledon or a bicycle in the Tour de France, more has to be done than simply loan a product to be a sponsor.

Endorsement

Paying the same competitor to say why he or she uses your product is product endorsement, not sponsorship. A sponsor will be meeting the expenses of the competitor or the team, and perhaps more.

Charitable donations

Just as individuals make donations to a charity without regard for any direct benefit to themselves, companies do so without expecting a commercial return. Companies can find that there is a community relations aspect to making a charitable donation. There can even be adverse community relations implications for any company that becomes known as ungenerous.

Companies find that well-targeted charitable donations will also have a beneficial effect on the way in which their employees view them. It is not unknown for companies to involve their employees with their charitable activities. NatWest for example, has a policy of matching charitable donations raised by its employees pound for pound.

The charities supported by business concerns cover a wide spectrum, including medical research and those that aid deprived sections of society. Companies will also donate funds to charities concerned with animal welfare, the environment or the nation's heritage. Many will favour charities that are local to their areas of business.

Not all claimants for assistance will be registered as charities. Individual requests for assistance or the work of some preservation societies sometimes fall outside the scope of registration. This does not inhibit some companies from supporting such activities, however.

Many artistic events and activities have achieved charitable status. However, for the purposes of a sponsorship programme, these really need to be regarded as sponsorship rather than a charitable donation. This is because supporting an artistic event is almost invariably a sponsorship. Donations to support the general running of the arts organisation itself might be construed as a charitable donation for tax purposes.

Political parties are not regarded as being charitable concerns, and donations have to be accounted for separately.

Community Sponsorship

This is one of the fastest-growing areas of sponsorship, and is often indistinguishable from social sponsorship. Sponsoring bottle banks with the organisation's name on the side could be a form of community sponsorship, but it could also be advertising, or good community relations.

The relative absence of 'company towns' in the UK has meant that business provision of amenities such as libraries or schools is less common than in some countries. Nevertheless, companies have been known to support the provision of swimming baths and sports centres, and the restoration of old canals or railway lines for example.

Social Sponsorship

The hybrid between sponsorship and a charitable donation is social sponsorship, which can also take many forms. The difference between social sponsorship and a charitable donation is that the sponsor expects the full range of sponsorship benefits. In contrast to most sponsorship, the social sponsorship activity is expected to meet certain social needs, whether it be the provision of an amenity or supporting a fund-raising event.

Cherry Blossom, the shoe polish manufacturer, sponsored the Scouts' traditional 'Bob-a-Job Week', which centred around offering a shoeshine service to the public. This met several objectives – raising product awareness and encouraging people to take an interest in the upkeep and appearance of their footwear. Providing the raw materials for the exercise meant that Cherry Blossom underwrote the costs of the fund-raising activity.

Finding social sponsorship opportunities that have a profile in direct relationship to their cost is not easy. A housing charity offered sponsorship of an extra floor in a block of flats in return for a mention on the board showing the charity's name and that of its contractors. Not surprisingly, sponsorship was not forthcoming. The cost did not justify the profile because few of those passing would have noticed the name of a sponsor, and even fewer would have been influenced by it.

Social sponsorship can materialise as an extension of an existing sponsorship programme. A good example of this arises when a major sports sponsorship can be extended to include events for young people or the disabled. Alternatively, an arts sponsorship can be extended to provide opportunities for school children to attend a play or an exhibition. These activities can be taken to remote areas away from the major cities, providing access to the arts for those in rural communities.

Those concerned with social sponsorship have to beware of creating offence. Appearing to take advantage of those in need or making use of pensioners or children are possible causes. Those benefiting from the work of a charity must not be the target audience for any social sponsorship, unless organisations such as the National Trust or its Scottish counterpart are being considered.

Nevertheless, social sponsorship is possible and does offer opportunities. However, it will entail more effort from the sponsor than the more traditional commercial sponsorships with organisers long accustomed to the needs and expectations of business sponsors.

SPONSORSHIP AND CHARITABLE DONATIONS TODAY

The growing overlap between sponsorship and charitable donations is one of the changes that have been taking place in recent years. Others have included the growing use of sponsorship by the tobacco industry. Sponsorship for programmes broadcast on independent radio and television in the UK has also been introduced. Charities have seen the addition of major media events to their other fund-raising activities.

The overlap of sponsorship and charitable donations has largely been the outcome of the trend towards what has become known as 'social sponsorship'. This is the sponsorship of projects that aid charitable efforts. These include fund-raising, those having a beneficial impact on the environment, heritage, job-creation, or in the provision of amenities.

Social sponsorship.

A certain amount of controversy has arisen because much of the pressure for social sponsorship has come from the Government. Many business leaders take the view that this is unacceptable, seeing their role in supporting charities as extending the work of government, not replacing it.

The ban on television advertising of tobacco products has forced many of the tobacco companies into the sponsorship of major televised sporting events, especially motor racing. Opposition is growing to the televising of events that are either sponsored by the tobacco industry, or which feature competitors sponsored by the tobacco industry. If such a ban occurs there will be a substantial fall in the volume of sponsorship. This could lead to difficulties for many organisers of events, and for many sports such as motor racing, which have become heavily dependent on tobacco advertising.

It is always possible that some other consumer product will be ostracised, driven off the television screens and forced to turn to sponsorship as an alternative. Alcohol could be one of these, but it might be difficult for the manufacturers or importers of alcoholic drinks to sponsor motor racing because of the unwelcome link between drinking and driving.

Many believe that sports sponsorship has been overdone and that too much money has been given. The large number of generous sponsors has also meant that the clash between conflicting sponsors has reduced the value of sporting sponsorship. The events, the competitors or teams, and the organisers are now seen as being too greedy.

The growth of programme sponsorship.

In recent years, the rules that banned programme sponsorship in Britain have been relaxed. Although still confined to independent radio and television, and to cable or satellite programmes, a growing number of programmes have been sponsored.

The rules prevent sponsors from supporting television programmes directly involved with their business, or from interfering with the freedom of producers or editors. These restrictions are not as onerous or self-defeating as they might appear. Barclaycard has been able to sponsor a television travel programme even though many people will pay for their holidays with a credit card. An airline, a ferry operator or a tour operator would not be allowed to sponsor such a programme.

In practice, some of the rules surrounding radio programme sponsorship appear to be less limiting. A stockbroker could, for example, provide a review of the week's share price movements.

Most of the programmes sponsored so far have been popular or light entertainment. Nevertheless, more heavyweight programmes such as radio stock market reports are relatively inexpensive to produce and can offer good value for the smaller sponsor. There is no direct link between the cost of making a programme and the cost of sponsorship – this is a matter for negotiation.

Apart from social sponsorship, charities have also seen changes in recent years. No longer are they solely dependent on donations from individuals or companies, on grants and legacies, or fund-raising events such as dinners. Taking their lead from the United States, the media have created a number of major fund-raising events for charities including Comic Relief, the BBC's Children in Need appeal and ITV's Telethon. These have shown how fund-raising can operate on a major scale. They appeal to individuals, companies, and stimulate groups of people who belong to the same club, drink in the same pub, or work for the same company to undertake fund-raising events. The Children in Need appeal alone raised £27 million in 1991, but more recently the donations have fallen, either because of economic recession, boredom, or a reaction to so many demands on the public.

Charities and change.

There have also been special one-off events such as releasing records or the organisation of concerts for famine relief. Underwriting the costs of these activities is one form of social sponsorship for companies.

Although the opportunities for sponsorship and charitable donations have grown and changed, a full understanding of these activities has eluded many managements. Companies engage in these activities simply because they feel they should do something, or because their competitors do.

Lord Leverhulme once said: 'I know that half the money I spend on advertising is wasted, and the trouble is I don't know which half.' Many businessmen might say the same thing about their sponsorship budgets. Careful analysis might show that more than half the money was being wasted.

Many still do not know what sponsorship is, what it can and can't do, or what it should cost. The confusion of businessmen who buy an allocation of seats at a concert or a rugby match and describe this as sponsorship rather than corporate hospitality should not be forgotten. Corporate hospitality can be an element within sponsorship as can advertising. Equally, too many believe that having negotiated a sponsorship agreement, they have done all that is necessary to ensure success. The truth is that much more needs to be done in addition to the basic sponsorship, both in terms of expenditure and effort, to make it work.

CHECKLIST

- What are your company's major sponsorships?
- How do these relate to your company's business, its marketing and to its key target audiences?
- What other activities are linked into the sponsorship, such as hospitality and advertising?
- Is corporate hospitality the prime element in the sponsorship, or simply a part of it?
- Does your company make charitable donations, and if so, who are the main beneficiaries?
- Are there charities which could have a natural connection with your business?
- Do charities offer a business development opportunity through social sponsorship?

Chapter 2
The Role of Corporate Support

Before delving deeper into the management of sponsorship and charitable donations – the 'corporate support' of your employer or your client – it is worth considering exactly why companies indulge in these activities. It is not enough to say glibly that it 'raises the profile' or 'creates local goodwill'. Still less satisfactory is the explanation that 'other companies do it', because success in marketing often lies in being different and, perhaps even more important, being perceived as being different.

Companies operate primarily in the interests of their shareholders who are encouraged to invest their money rather than leaving it in a building society account. The inducement is the dual prospect of **Profits and values.** receiving a share of the profits in the form of a dividend, and of the growth of the company, which takes the form of a capital gain on their shares. No profit means no investment, and ultimately no company. Your freedom to manage, advise and implement a course of action depends on the continued independence of the company, or even on its survival.

Those business enterprises that do not have shareholders in the normal sense, the mutual institutions such as building societies and some life assurance offices, need profits to maintain an adequate capital base. Without it their regulator will either close them or, more likely, seek a merger with another stronger institution. The only way such institutions can expand and grow is by retaining profits and converting these into reserves.

So, profits are important. In which case, why do companies provide funds for sponsorship? Even if one accepts that this is another means of promoting the business, and ultimately increasing profits, why do 99 per cent of British companies give money away to charities?

The reasons for these actions are varied. Companies are run by people and have a distinctive character or culture that reflects human values in their actions. Corporate as well as individual motives can vary. The reasons for companies undertaking a particular project can range from outright charity through to a carefully calculated plan to be seen to be doing the right thing in order to achieve a particular corporate aim. Never be surprised if you discover that one company is altruistic and concerned with its role in the community, whereas another is inclined to take a hard-headed approach. There is also an attitude that can be best described as 'enlightened self-interest'.

There are many organisers of sponsored events or activities who genuinely believe that companies sponsor because it is a nice thing to do. These are the same people who believe that they do not have to do anything to please the sponsor, for whom sending a cheque is a privilege. The truth is that the general public show a strong correlation between familiarity with a company and favourability towards it, as Figure 2.1 shows. Not all audiences follow this pattern, as we see in Figure 2.2 showing the more demanding approach of personal finance journalists.

THE RELATIONSHIP BETWEEN BUSINESS AND THE COMMUNITY

Sponsorship is not always aimed wholly at a single target audience, neither are charitable donations. Companies also endeavour to influence other audiences whose approval can improve a company's prospects. These opinion formers include journalists and politicians as well as others in a position of prominence and influence.

Listening to the opinion formers.

The British Market Research Bureau conducted a survey on 'The Social Responsibilities of Major Corporations'. It was based on interviews with senior business people, prominent business editors and journalists, and the leaders of major trade unions. The survey investigated corporate sponsorship of the arts and sport, as well as charitable donations and support for community projects. It also

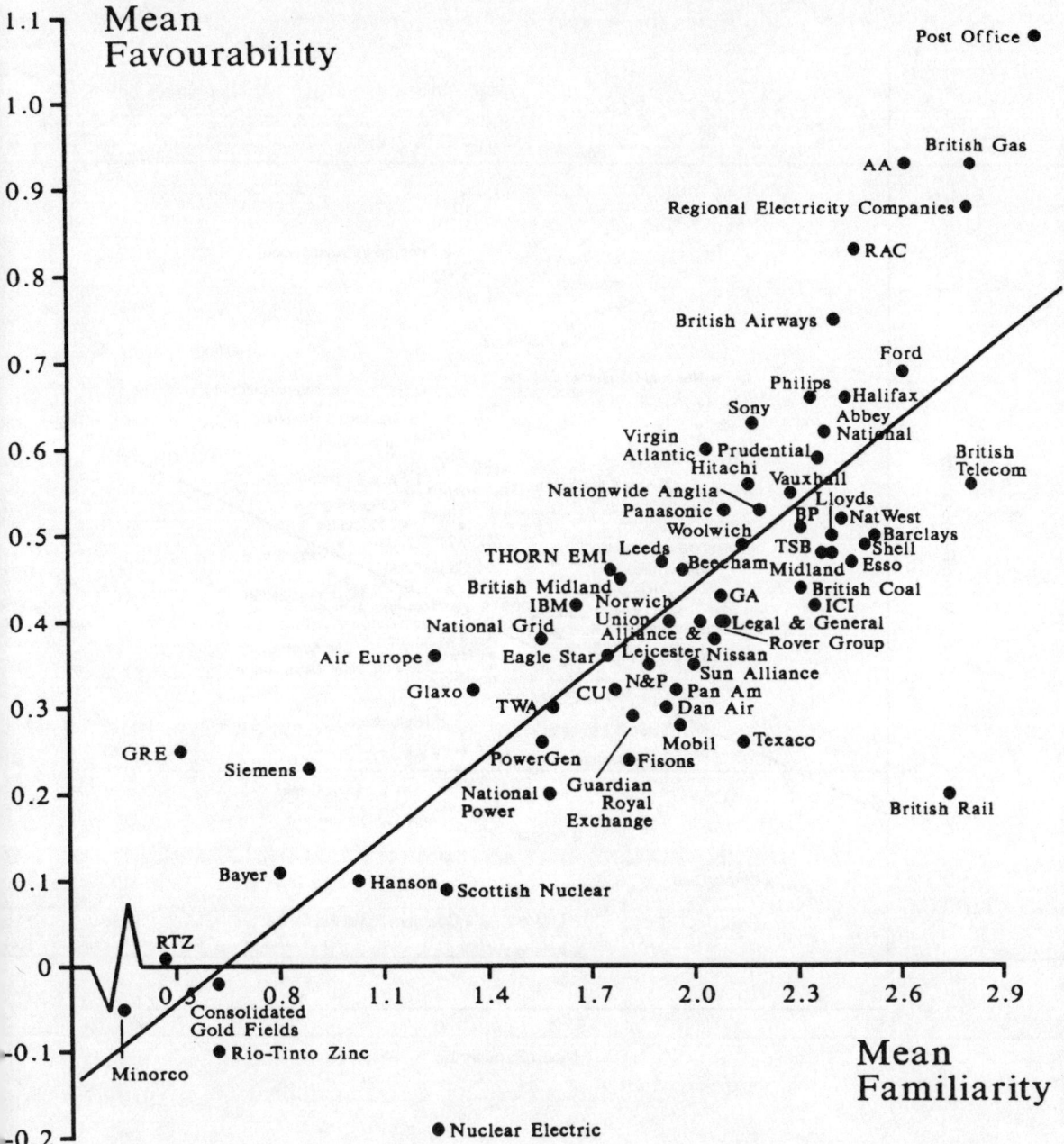

Figure 2.1   In surveys of the general public, there is usually high correlation between familiarity and favourability.

Base: All   **Source: MORI**

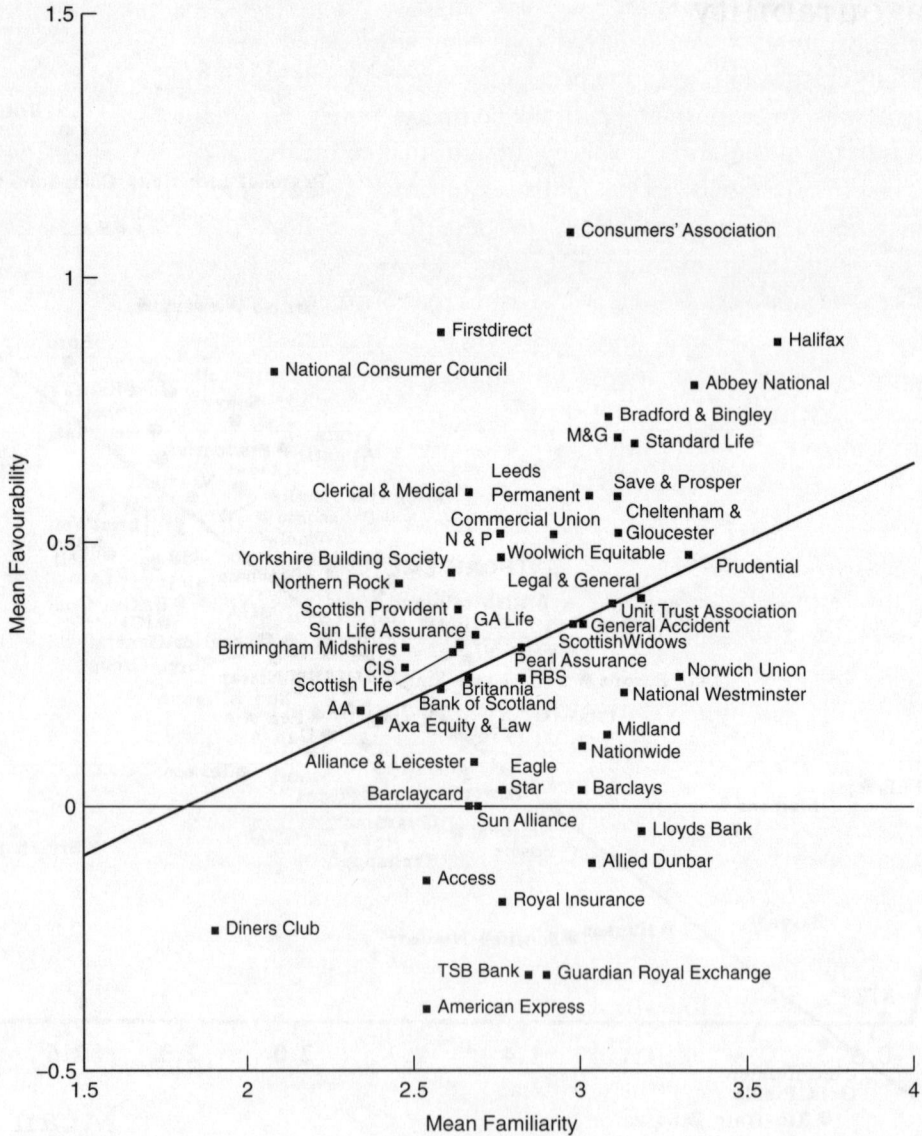

Figure 2.2   Audiences who know an industry well, tend to behave in the opposite way to the general public, with no correlation between familiarity and favourability, as this survey of personal finance journalists shows.

Base: All respondents   Source: MORI

covered some of the reasons for companies providing financial support for worthy projects.

Most of those interviewed believed that companies acted out of commercial interest as one would expect, but more than half also felt that altruism was an important factor in company policy on such matters. A quarter of those in the survey thought that companies also hoped to inspire staff with pride in the company. Trades union leaders were more likely than other respondents to believe that companies acted out of humanitarian reasons.

The consensus among those interviewed was that business support for community projects was of immense value to the public. Three-quarters of them believed that sponsored activities would not survive without business support.

Individual businesses have different perspectives on sponsorship and charitable donations, and although there are occasions when the dividing line is blurred, or even erased, the perspectives should first be understood.

Glaxo, the major British pharmaceutical manufacturer, has a clear view of why it provides support for charities and in sponsoring community projects.

'Charitable and community participation is an important aspect of business practice since companies do not operate in a vacuum or within an exclusive business environment', according to the Chairman, Sir Paul Girolami. 'Industrial and commercial activities are essential components of communities and share with them a social responsibility.

The idea that an enterprise, in placing its priority on efficiency, can ignore the community in which it operates, is unsound. A company has to recognise that the framework provided by the community is an essential ingredient in the efficient operation of the business'.

Sir Paul's belief is that an industrial activity can only do its job well if it forms part of an open, educated and healthy society.

'As a result, a company must go beyond providing jobs and a demand for services; it has to promote and sustain such a society by participating in community operations as a member of that community'.

SPONSORSHIP

A wise company sponsors in order to achieve definite commercial objectives. All companies should be realistic about their sponsorship aims, even if they are not always too commercially-minded about it.

Unfortunately, the belief that companies sponsor the chairman's or chief executive's favourite hobby has more than a grain of truth about it. One building society sponsored Friesian cows, and that at a time when building societies were not allowed to undertake commercial lending! The reason for this support was that breeding Friesian cattle was the chairman's hobby.

Most companies have no idea why they sponsor. This is largely because the 'sponsorship' is either an act of self-indulgence, the end result of political or municipal coercion, or simple corporate hospitality. In fact, companies become involved in sponsorship for three main reasons.

Name awareness, or image

Most businesses wish to raise their profile, sometimes with a particular audience. This led Cornhill Insurance to sponsor test cricket, and Barclays Bank to sponsor football. Cornhill found that awareness of their name rose dramatically as a result of their sponsorship, but the new-found awareness was among an audience that was predominantly male and enthusiastic about cricket. As their target audience matched the characteristics of this group, the exercise was a complete success.

Product promotion

This is dear to the heart of every marketing professional, many of whom would suggest that all sponsorship exercises should be for this purpose. In the case of a bank or an insurance company, sponsorship that promotes the name will often reflect well on the product range. However, companies that are heavily brand orientated, the alcoholic drinks, tobacco and confectionery industries, (and detergents and washing up materials although these seldom sponsor), need to advertise the brand or the product. Added impetus is given to this type of sponsorship by the tight restrictions on tobacco products advertising in the UK.

Corporate hospitality

Entertaining important customers, agents, distributors, professional connections, or even suppliers of some standing, is an important element in business life. Other important audiences meriting hospitality include the media, investment analysts and the investment or fund managers of major institutional investors. However, these audiences tend to be entertained less frequently, possibly because they are smaller groups, or because of the number of invitations they receive.

It is possible to combine corporate hospitality with either of the two preceding categories of sponsorship, and it is possible to entertain without sponsoring as one can see at sporting fixtures and artistic events.

THE SPONSOR'S EXPECTATIONS

What are the major benefits of a sponsorship package? Much depends on the individual opportunity, but the most common include:

Tickets

This should be elementary, but the sponsorship package should always include an agreed number of tickets for guests of the sponsor. This does not mean that you simply have to consider the cost of the sponsorship and expect tickets to the full value of the sponsorship (there might not be enough seats), but expect a realistic number as part of the package. A rugby sponsorship can include a hundred tickets for a major game, a ballet performance may offer less than this.

In addition, a number of tickets could be made available at reduced cost for employees, customers, or other audiences of interest to the sponsor such as school children. This is usually less easy to arrange with sporting events, but stage productions can offer discounted tickets for those performances that are likely to attract less than capacity audiences.

The provision of tickets for dress rehearsals for employees or their families can also enhance the value of the sponsorship. They must understand though that a dress rehearsal is not a performance and may be neither perfect, nor even on time.

Programme Mentions

The name of the sponsor, or principal sponsor, should be mentioned in the programme with a sponsor's message. There should also be at least one advertisement in a prominent position such as on the back cover. The title page of the programme must also state that the event is 'Sponsored by ...'. If minor sponsors are involved, these can be listed. The ideal is for the sponsor not to allow competitors or near-competitors to advertise in the same programme. An example of a near-competitor would be a bank sponsoring an event not allowing a building society to advertise.

Name Awareness

Name awareness is a commodity in increasing demand among sponsors. The name can be that of the sponsoring company as in the Barclays League, or the Whitbread Round-the-World Yacht Race. Or it can be a brand, such as Barclaycard's sponsorship of a television travel programme or the Nescafé sponsorship of the Radio Chart Show on the Independent Radio Network.

This desire among sponsors to incorporate their name in the title of an event often results in a highly pragmatic approach. There are events clearly branded with the name of the sponsor, such as the Cornhill Tests, the Barclays' League and Bristol & West Bowls, but there are many other events, especially in the arts, which are not treated in this way. This is not to say that the sponsorship should be hidden, but the name of the organisation can be shown by having posters and other material, including tickets, clearly marked 'sponsored by ...'. There are examples such as the 'Daily Mail Ideal Home Exhibition' but alternatively, the 'Royal Highland Show' simply has as a sub-heading 'Principal Sponsor – The Royal Bank of Scotland'.

The extent to which name awareness has to be taken should not be under-estimated. At a sporting event, the sponsors can expect to see advertisements at the ground, their name on posters, tickets, inside the programmes, and on the shirts or the number cards of the players or competitors.

At an art exhibition, concert, ballet, or other production of the performing arts, posters can be expected to mention the main sponsor by name. This will also apply to programmes and tickets, reinforcing the association in the minds of the customers. Sponsors can advertise their sponsorship, especially in arts or sporting publications and the supplements produced by the daily and Sunday press. However, if the normal product advertising can simply carry a sponsorship design or brand logo, then the space is not wasted and the product message is not detracted from in any way.

Sponsorship Branding

It is increasingly common for major sponsorships to develop their own branding, sometimes incorporating the name or branding of the sponsor. In golf, Toyota used a branding depicting a stylised golfer, balancing their own logo on opposite sides of the signage. Stella Artois with tennis, and Alfa Romeo with polo, incorporated their own logotypes into the sponsorship design.

The object of the exercise is to increase awareness of the association between the brand and the event, not simply to remind those attending or watching the event that it has been sponsored. The introduction of sponsorship branding enables the sponsors to use the sponsorship brand in their own product advertising, again reinforcing the connection in the mind of the customer.

Advertising

The advertising by a sponsor proclaiming their involvement with an event is really a matter for the sponsor, not the organiser, but the organisers can be expected to mention the sponsor in any advertising for the event.

It is important that the sponsor is able to advertise and be given, as part of the package, prime positions in programmes and at the locations for any sponsored event. Sponsors should always expect to provide a sponsorship message in programmes, this takes the form of a brief message from the chairman or chief executive of the sponsoring business.

Hospitality and Entertainment

At most major sponsorships, the sponsors will expect a corporate hospitality or entertainment opportunity to be available, although they can often make such arrangements themselves. Companies that need to entertain and are not interested in the broader sponsorship package, should be encouraged to view their role as a minor sponsor or simply a supporter. Never be hesitant about asking for such a package for corporate entertainment if that is all your company wants. This will cost much less than sponsorship, but still expect to pay a premium price.

In many cases, sponsors make their own hospitality arrangements, perhaps having a marquee at a racecourse or a sports field. Alternatively, a meal or drinks can be provided at a venue away from the location of the sponsorship before or after (or even before and after) the sponsored event. Always check whether the organisers can provide facilities at the event, and what they will cost as you might obtain lower prices and better quality through making your own arrangements.

Special Opportunities

The private viewing or the preview of an art exhibition is something special that sponsors and their guests may seldom experience. People like a feeling of exclusivity, of being able to wander around an exhibition with a drink in their hand and not being bothered by crowds, or even worse, crowds of rowdy school children on an outing.

Such opportunities are not confined to the arts. There are other possibilities, including allowing sponsors an evening for their guests to view a building of architectural or historic importance that has been restored with the support of the sponsor, or in summer an evening at a zoo or a botanical garden.

Personal Appearances

Sponsorship enables the sponsor to invite guests who are both important for the sponsor's business and interested in the occasion or the event. One can go a step beyond this, delighting your guests with an opportunity to meet performers or sportsmen at a meal or drinks afterwards. The personal appearance should be by the stars, and not necessarily an opportunity for everyone in the team or in the cast to appear.

Many sponsors now can expect stars or members of sponsored sporting teams to be available for branch openings or as after dinner speakers. The thoughtful sponsor will appreciate that many performers have other commitments, including rehearsals, and sportsmen and women have to train. Many athletes have a regular job as well, sometimes with an employer who will provide time off for training and travel for away matches, but who is unlikely to view sponsorship appearances in the same light.

Be realistic while remaining aware of the possibilities. The captain of a professional football team or an actor can be available for a personal appearance with a little planning. It is important to remember both that many leading personalities in sport and in the arts can command high fees for personal appearances, and that they are capable of resenting being taken advantage of by an insensitive sponsor.

Advertising Support

In addition to the personal appearances, sponsors can use members of the cast of a stage production or team members in their advertising. This is a possibility that should be considered at the negotiating stage, and the fees agreed. There is a potential difficulty with amateur athletes, especially if one of them works for a competitor of the sponsor!

Mailing Lists

Many organisers of sponsored events have extensive mailing lists, including subscribers and members. The sponsor's involvement can be made known in any routine mailings of newsletters or programmes, and the sponsor should consider asking for promotional material to be included in such mailings. However, the extra costs of postage and stuffing envelopes needs to be borne in mind.

It might be possible to let the sponsor have the use of the mailing list, but the legal position should be checked first. In some countries, legislation such as Britain's Data Protection Act can have a bearing on the transfer of such information.

Promotional Items

It is usual for sponsors to invest in items such as T-shirts, golf umbrellas, funny hats, and the other paraphernalia that glories under the name of 'promotional items'. Some of these items are rubbish and risk insulting the recipient, but others can be useful or even stylish. It helps if the promotional item has some relevance to the event – golf umbrellas at a golf sponsorship are an obvious example, but you can always go a step further and have smaller ladies' golfing umbrellas as well.

Sometimes production runs can be extended and unit costs reduced if promotional items are good enough to be offered for sale to members or supporters of the sponsored activity. Even your own company's employees can be offered the opportunity to buy, which will cut down cadging and the temptation to pilfer!

Employee involvement

The possibility of providing tickets for employees has already been mentioned, but there are other opportunities as well. Smaller companies who might support a local football team may well find that employees' enthusiasm for following the team also leads to an appreciation of the company's action in providing support.

Customer involvement

Although major customers will be guests and enjoy the corporate hospitality of sponsorship, retailers and manufacturers of consumer products can use other ways to involve customers in a sponsorship. Competitions can reflect the theme of the sponsorship, for example.

Durability

Sponsors hope that their association with the event will linger on long after the sponsorship has ended. This is hard to achieve, especially when some long running sponsorships produce diminishing returns for the sponsor. Nevertheless, it can happen, especially with community projects and in such fields as education and scientific research. If one is fortunate in sponsoring an individual who eventually achieves fame and glory, this may lead to media coverage that mentions the name of the early sponsor. On the other hand, individuals are high risk.

From this collection of opportunities it can be seen that sponsorship offers a wide range of benefits. Even if your company has products or brands that can be readily promoted using other means, sponsorship will often provide an additional opportunity. The media are mainly interested in news, and a product or a brand that has been on the market for many years with little or no change has little opportunity for media exposure on its own. A high profile sponsorship can change that by providing ample mentions of the sponsor's name, as long as the message reaches the right audience!

Sponsorship can also offer flexibility. Perhaps your company has a small target audience, and you can reach them through sponsoring a suitable activity. You might opt for a lower profile sponsorship, and one that is less expensive. Television coverage, for example, might not be necessary, or even desirable. Alternatively, you must be careful not to pay for sponsorship when a good quality and well-targeted corporate hospitality exercise might do instead.

The important task for those responsible for promoting a company and with control over sponsorship, is to ensure that your employers, or your clients, are fully aware of their expectations from sponsorship, and that their objectives are well-defined. Good name promotion from sponsorship is difficult, and it is expensive. The basic rule is that as much is spent on promotion of the sponsorship as on the sponsorship itself. This includes entertainment, promotional items (golf umbrellas, ties, and other paraphernalia), and advertising. Depending on the circumstances, you might spend more, or less.

If the real idea behind a sponsorship is to entertain guests, then businesses can negotiate an entertainment facility for less than the direct costs of sponsorship. The added advantage is that they will not have to provide for additional items such as advertising the sponsorship. Rather than spending massive sums on sponsoring sporting events, the purchase of debentures providing the right to certain seats, or other arrangements, can guarantee good quality hospitality opportunities at a fraction of the cost.

A basic principle for the discerning sponsor, if the idea is to publicise the company or a brand, is that sponsorship should never be shared. One hopes that a sponsorship will attract favourable publicity. However, it is difficult enough to ensure that media coverage will mention the name of a single major sponsor let alone the name of two or more; the same applies to programmes and other printed material. It is difficult to provide adequate space for more than one sponsor, unless one wishes to submerge the public in a welter of names.

One sometimes sees the names of joint sponsors in the foyer of an opera house or concert hall. The plaque containing the names is unnoticed by the majority of those passing through, and the collection of names means that no one company stands out or is remembered. Sometimes the names are repeated in a list in programmes, but again, the only people likely to bother with the list are the employees of a sponsoring company.

CHARITABLE DONATIONS

Many companies feel that they should support charities. This is not because of any right on the part of any charity to have access to company funds, but because most company managements and their shareholders have a conscience and a desire to do the right thing.

The individual's own sense of generosity has its corporate counterpart because companies are comprised of people, managed by them and owned by them. This sense of what is right extends to most companies not actively seeking publicity for their charitable activities. However, opportunities will arise to invite the media when a substantial donation is made, or major support spread over a number of years is announced.

There are limits to generosity, of course. If your company is making large losses, perhaps closing factories and making staff redundant, there might be the view that charity begins at home. Any company making substantial donations to charity while laying off workers is likely to be compared with those wealthy Victorians who would contribute towards missionary work in Africa, while neglecting their own household servants or tenants.

Nevertheless, previously agreed long-term commitments must be honoured, and it might only be necessary to maintain the charitable donations budget at the previous year's level rather than cut it. Alternatively, in a difficult period, it is permissible to become more selective over donations.

With both sponsorship and donations, companies must avoid controversy. It doesn't mix well with business, and in the case of some charities it risks offending customers or even employees.

To make the best use of the available funds, companies must sometimes consider how to restrict their donations. Otherwise they can become mere postboxes processing appeals and providing a token amount in response. In some cases this can be easy. Many years ago the author worked for a shipowner, whose generosity was concentrated on maritime charities. This helped seafarers in distress or their dependants, and the Royal National Lifeboat Institution. The result was that substantial donations could be made to each, and on one occasion a new lifeboat was paid for. Few companies have such a clear-cut choice, even though it also makes administration easier and less expensive.

The problem is still more difficult for businesses that have a substantial branch network, which both raises their profile amongst charity-fund raisers and enlarges the area over which their largesse must be dispersed. Banks have genuine problems in concentrating funds in any one area. They not only have a large branch network, they are also involved in all areas of business, with every activity needing a bank account. They could not afford to take the attitude of a shipowner and focus their support on just one type of charity.

As with sponsorship, many companies adopt the one easy means available to them of reducing the demands on the charities budget. This is to support charities only if they operate in those geographical areas in which the organisation has a business presence. Small local charities will still tackle the local branch of any organisation with a substantial branch network.

Defining a policy.

As mentioned in Chapter 1, there is a dislike among many in the business community of seeing their charitable donations being used to compensate for a lack of government funding. Individuals probably take the same view. Businesses, and their employees, pay their taxes and work in an often difficult economic climate. Charitable donations provide an opportunity for generosity, and to express an interest in a particular activity or area of need. Donors do not want to compensate for the shortcomings of government, local or national, or for mal-administration.

This is another way of defining a policy for charitable donations. Business will not usually fund education or health, although specific appeals including medical research will usually be sympathetically considered. Business is happy to extend the work of government, but not to replace it.

There are fashions in charitable donations. In recent years, support for environmental matters has been growing, so too has support for anything connected with training or retraining.

Some companies have more than one fund so that, for example, items connected with the country's heritage, employment generation or the environment, are supported by new funds over and above those created for charitable purposes.

Organisations such as the Per Cent Club encourage companies publicly to commit themselves to giving a percentage of their divi-dends each year to charitable and other worthy causes. The term 'other worthy causes' reflects the fact that not all recipients are officially registered charities. Some would find it difficult to achieve registration: railway and canal preservation societies are seldom, if ever, charities. The same goes for those restoring old mills, but not those restoring church towers, therefore many businesses prefer to overlook the distinction and still provide support.

The problems with religious appeals.

On the other hand, corporate support for religious appeals, whe-ther restoration projects or missionary work, is falling. At present, it is difficult to be sure whether this is a reflection of a rising num-ber of church restoration projects having flooded the market, and compelled companies to take the view that it is easier to say 'no' to them all, or simply a reflection of the increasing secularisation of society.

The reluctance to consider appeals from the churches could reflect the growing irritation of the business community with constant cri-ticism of business by church leaders. This is a growing problem for church-based charities, and one that cannot be dismissed lightly because such irritation is most acute among those who are regular church-goers and who do strive to follow their faith in making their business decisions. Much of the criticism by the clergy of business is based on a lack of understanding, but worse still, some of it is wholly inaccurate and even untruthful.

Events such as charity dinners are decreasing in popularity, not only because they are extremely expensive, and the corporate hospitality element is usually overplayed, but because relatively little of the sums paid will find their way to the charity in question.

Some companies dislike advertising in publications produced by charities, including programmes for example, but this is less clear cut. Some charities do need to have companies advertising in their publications, thereby demonstrating that they have the support of some of the leading names in British business and are to be taken seriously. This is also the author's attitude, but it also means that charity advertising is a small part of the overall budget and deliberately so.

Much depends on the publication; many businesses could make a commercial case for advertising in the National Trust magazine, or even in the RNLI publication. One charity in the UK, Help the Aged, mounted a fund-raising campaign sponsored by an insurance company, Eagle Star. Other businesses would take a different view, and not provide money specifically for fund-raising.

It is not just the cost of advertising in charity programmes and the poor return to the charity concerned that rankles. Many of the so-called 'professionals' are amateurish in the way they pester companies unduly. It is not uncommon for a dozen telephone calls to be received at a company as a team of 'telephone salespeople' works through a list. They all attempt to talk down the charities coordinator without once considering whether or not they are repeating the efforts of a colleague a day or two, or just an hour or two, earlier!

When considering an ad hoc advertising opportunity, you will often wish to have the technical details, such as page size, to help in making a decision. It is easier to decide to take an advertisement if existing artwork will fit. In the case of many charity publications, the reaction to this request is often to explain that such material does not exist, instead they will send you an order confirmation!

Charities use a mixture of paid and voluntary help in raising funds. Clearly, the small local charity is completely dependent on voluntary help, but larger charities will always include at least a core of professional fund-raisers. Whether or not you are dealing with a professional should not influence your judgement.

Charities seeking sponsorship are often unable to offer the sponsorship benefits that a sponsor might expect. In the case of a charity seeking help with the purchase of a vehicle, there is the difficulty that high utilisation is required for high exposure, which can mean poor condition and a downgraded message being conveyed. Far better to write-off such exercises as a donation.

Underwriting the cost of a performance or a sporting event for a charity can be one way of combining charitable support and sponsorship, possibly even adding corporate hospitality to the mix. Even so, this is only worth doing if the event is of sufficiently high quality, and that one can be assured that money is not going into the pockets of performers or competitors, or the organisers.

Inevitably, with more than 170,000 charities in England and Wales alone, there are many charities that are registered but are not sufficiently well regulated by the overburdened Charity Commissioners. The experienced administrators of charitable funds soon become aware of these and avoid them.

CHECKLIST

- Check your company's sponsorshiip activities to see how many of the criteria referred to on pages 24–5 they meet.
- How many of the additional items mentioned are coupled with the sponsorship? If any are missing, why have they not been added?
- Are any of your sponsorships shared? If so, why? Are there any advantages in this, other than cost?
- Are the charitable donations confined to an area or a particular need? If not, could this be done?
- Does your company buy charitable advertising, or participate in charity dinners? Is there any alternative that could increase the benefit to the charity?
- Are there any sponsorshiip opportunities arising from your charity connections that could help the charity and assist the business?

Chapter 3

Matching Activity to the Corporate Objectives

There is now a greater variety of sponsorship opportunities than at any time in the past. It is no longer a case of a sponsor choosing between sport and the arts, or even a community project. Today the sponsor can also consider television programmes, university facilities, books and other publications, as well as schools and hospitals. In Britain, a bus company advertised for sponsorship although without success!

The same can be said about charitable support. The number of charities has mushroomed, reaching more than 170,000 in England and Wales. Although donations are as welcome as ever, many charities realise they can do better by offering some form of sponsorship opportunity instead.

Although the opportunities have been growing, the funds available have not been keeping pace. This is true despite the substantial injection of funds into sponsorship in the UK resulting from the ban on tobacco advertising on television. This has forced the tobacco industry to divert the substantial funds available for television advertising into sponsorship. Such windfalls are a one-off addition to the total available expenditure. Such funds might disappear at short notice if restrictions are introduced to make it more difficult for the names of tobacco industry sponsors to be shown or mentioned in broadcast coverage of sport.

An imbalance has arisen over the years. Sports sponsorship has swallowed most of the available funds, and the organisers of the more popular, higher profile, sporting events have become accustomed to stretching the generosity of the main sponsors. Arts sponsorship has been less popular and has received around one-sixth of the funds devoted to sport. Community projects and social sponsorship have been even less well funded. The introduction of sponsorship for independent, cable and satellite television programmes as well as independent radio, will further increase the competition for sponsorship funds.

This growing competition for business support must be good for those entrusted with controlling a sponsorship budget. The massive proportion of the available sponsorship funds devoted to sport has more than simply inflated the expectations of organisers. It has meant that sport has become saturated with sponsors making it more difficult for each new sponsor's message to stand out from the general 'noise' level.

Sport is not alone in this. Although the arts, of all kinds, have not fared nearly as well as sport in the proportion of the overall funds received, there are localised exceptions. Some major arts festivals, such as those held in Edinburgh and Bath, are so big that a single event will attract very little media attention. Good media coverage is difficult to achieve at these festivals because the small and select cadre of critics is unable to cover everything. The media space is not available because newspapers cannot expand their theatre and other performing arts coverage dramatically for a few weeks each year.

Unfortunately, the cost to sponsors of supporting a performance at such festivals is considerably higher than for quality events held elsewhere. These do not have to compete for the attention of reviewers or audiences whose appetites have been satiated by an artistic binge. Those who sponsor at such major events are engaged in a costly corporate hospitality exercise, and reap few of the other benefits normally available to a sponsor.

Considerable clarity of purpose is necessary for those responsible for guiding their company's sponsorship policy. It is difficult for the major sponsor to maintain the same benefits from each event or activity sponsored. If your company is the major sponsor of an orchestra, that sponsorship should extend for a reasonable period and include any performances at the festivals just mentioned. One simply has to accept that such performances are far worse value than an appearance before an appreciative audience in Norwich or Aberdeen.

The same can be argued for charitable donations. One needs to understand why a certain course of action is the right one. This is even more important if social sponsorship is contemplated. The best fit between an organisation and a social sponsorship is one that is comfortable and logical – a turkey breeder could hardly be expected to sponsor a competition for the best vegetarian recipe!

If the marketing or PR people cannot understand the justification behind sponsorship, they can hardly be expected to convince their colleagues in other disciplines. The interest aroused by many sponsorships means that the ability to carry others with you is more important than in many other activities. Even if the sponsorship reflects the interests of a particular director, doubts can remain unless the values and benefits can be presented clearly and concisely to the board.

Convincing colleagues and the board.

The absence of a suitable alternative explains why companies sometimes sponsor unsuitable events. Companies who feel that they ought to do something are at the mercy of whoever offers them a sponsorship opportunity simply because there is no worthwhile alternative.

There is another approach – if your company has a hard image then a sponsorship that shows it as caring or even as one with a 'cuddly' image could improve public perceptions.

FIVE STEPS TOWARDS THE RIGHT OPPORTUNITY

Matching the sponsorship opportunities to the organisation should not be difficult, providing that you use a methodical and slightly analytical approach, diligence, sensitivity, some creative management and common sense in approaching the problem. There is no great mystery in finding a suitable opportunity. The process consists of five simple steps:

❏ What would be the objective of sponsorship?
❏ Which audiences essential to the organisation's success would be reached through sponsorship?
❏ What activity or event is of most interest or concern to these audiences?
❏ Which geographical territories need to be covered?
❏ What is the desired image of the company, its products or brands?

These same criteria can be applied when sifting requests for charitable donations. Even if publicity is not being sought for the organisation's generosity and if the budget is limited (as it almost always is), it helps to lend some rationale to decisions if these factors are taken into account.

SPONSORSHIP OPPORTUNITIES

Not every sponsorship is going to be suitable. Just take a look at the possibilities open to you:

- ❑ Sporting events: Always popular with sponsors, and more likely to offer naming possibilities. Nevertheless, these are saturated with sponsors and the best opportunities rarely are available to the new sponsor.
- ❑ Artistic events: Usually lower profile, but will appeal to a particular type of customer or distributor, and more likely to appeal to both husband and wife than many sporting events. An added advantage is that most occur during the evening, which can make it easier for guests to attend.
- ❑ Local amenities, if the name of the sponsor can be incorporated into the name of the building, etc. Remember that such amenities can sometimes suffer over the years so either a continuing commitment is needed or assurances made that the building will not become shabby.
- ❑ Broadcast programmes, which are a recent innovation in the UK, but do not offer the sponsor a high profile on present rules. Although logos and trade names can now be screened, there is still the danger that this becomes so taken for granted that viewers will fail to notice it.
- ❑ Restoration projects, such as old railway locomotives, canals and so on, but these seldom offer a high enough profile for the costs involved.
- ❑ Environmental projects, which can include restoration, or underwriting the costs of such useful activities as recycling by providing bottle banks, etc, and perhaps meeting the costs of collection.

❑ Books, which although these are often low cost, they are also often low profile – unless they support marketing objectives.

❑ Newspapers and magazines sometimes seek sponsorship, including sponsorship of special supplements. This is usually another low profile activity with limited benefits.

❑ Education, including the endowment of a chair in a subject relevant to the company's business.

❑ Activities for young people, such as letter-writing contests.

❑ Conferences, although these have a limited benefit for the sponsors.

❑ Exhibitions, fairs or shows – providing that the sponsor's name is on publicity material as the main sponsor. It is often more cost-effective to sponsor an event at an exhibition or show than to sponsor the entire show.

Be wary of pitfalls inherent in some forms of sponsorship. The restrictions on sponsors influencing sponsored broadcasting have already been mentioned, but similar restrictions do not apply to sponsored publications. The end result is that a sponsored publication lacks credibility. One Scottish newspaper looks for bank sponsors for an occasional business magazine, but at least one bank has rejected this on the grounds that any criticism of a rival would be seen as having been influenced by their sponsorship. The same would also apply to any favourable mention of the sponsor's banking services – the entire value of editorial coverage is lost in this way.

Books can have similar shortcomings that cast doubt on the integrity of the contents. It can still be useful to consider a series of books relevant to your marketing objectives – a bank or building society could publish a book for first-time home buyers.

OBJECTIVES

Before planning any sponsorship, one should be clear about the objectives of the sponsorship; these will be the expectations that it will have to fulfil. This is important because careful analysis might suggest that sponsorship is not necessarily the best way forward. If your organisation has just twenty major customers worldwide, sponsorship aimed at them will be difficult to find and even more difficult to justify. However, if you have several million customers or potential customers in any particular territory, sponsorship may be an attractive proposition.

This assumes that impressing and influencing customers is the sole reason for the sponsorship, which might not be the case. Influencing customers could be a suitable additional benefit, but you might be more concerned with impressing potential and existing investors, or their advisors. The media might be an audience, as could politicians or members of pressure groups. You might want to make a favourable impression on potential and existing employees, or on the local community.

Sponsorship can only succeed if the company and its products have a sound reputation – sponsorship cannot overcome failings. If the corporate culture is flawed, sponsorship cannot compensate. If the products are poor, sponsorship will have been wasted. Sponsorship could even bring angry customers or investors in direct contact with the management!

Sponsorship and image.

Are you trying to sell the company's products or improve its image? One can argue that a good image is a prerequisite for successful selling, but companies often want a good image for other reasons. A company that is seen as environmentally aware is more likely to receive planning permission to build a new factory than one whose record is suspect. A company that is seen as being progressive and at the forefront of technology will be more attractive to school-leavers and bright graduates. Such a company will also be regarded as a good potential partner for other companies attracting offers of ideas, components and capital from the best possible sources.

THE AUDIENCE

It might appear that we have already touched on the subject of the audience, but audiences are more complex than any breakdown into customers, suppliers, politicians or investors might imply.

Companies are no longer simply concerned with relationships with customers. The very nature of public relations is to ensure good communication with all the audiences essential to a company's success. Publicly-quoted companies might for example, be anxious to sponsor something that interests investment analysts or the managers of their major institutional shareholders. Perhaps the time has come when such companies should identify a sponsorship proposition that will interest private shareholders!

A company that uses part of its sponsorship budget to ensure that the cost of tickets for the performing arts are brought within the reach of students could be doing one of several things. It might be interested in the students as customers now or in the future, or as potential employees. It might be endeavouring to please the parents of the students, the educational establishment, or the leaders of the community. Employees and prospective employees are sometimes borne in mind when sponsorship decisions are made.

Even in an era of increasing sexual equality, men and women have interests that may often overlap, but are not always the same. Many women are interested in motor racing and football, but the majority are not. Women are more likely to be interested in show jumping, tennis or fashion that men are. The number of single person households suggests that many men are likely to be interested in domestic matters, but they would still be outnumbered by women. The old stereotypes are not as marked as they used to be, but they are still relevant.

The objective might be to attract the interest of both men and women. This is completely realistic, especially if the subject is one that really does appeal to both. It might be that couples are more likely to be interested in an event that both of them can enjoy.

It follows that you must be sure of the breakdown of the audience by sex, age, region, social group, disposable income, and occupation. Research may be necessary if such information is not available, and there are companies who still know relatively little about their customers.

Analysing the audience.

One will often find branch or area managers who claim to know exactly what their audiences find of interest and they may well be right. But it is not unknown for such people to support sponsorships solely on the basis of what is of interest to them and their friends. Even if they have correctly identified something of interest to existing customers, they might be missing a larger and potentially more lucrative market by persisting with the same sponsorship and being oblivious to change.

ACTIVITY

The activity or event sponsored must appeal to the audience and be acceptable to the sponsor, as well as being a sensible match with its business and the objectives that have been defined.

Although one might enjoy the sponsored activity, it is more important that it is right for everyone else, the audience and one's employers rather than for oneself. It often happens that the sponsorship coordinator is handling a sponsorship in which he or she has little real interest. This is not always a bad thing because it can result in a more objective approach, but one must have at least a working knowledge of the area.

Evaluating the sponsorship.

Visibility is important, and can be related to value for money. It is not easy to evaluate one sponsorship compared to another, but two measures that can be helpful are:

❑ First, look at your competitors and their sponsorship programmes, evaluate just what they are doing and its costs. Does your management team feel that competitors are making an impact?
❑ Second, having decided on an arts, sport or community sponsorship, take a wider look at what others are doing in the field. What are they paying directly and indirectly to support the sponsorship and what are the results?

Judge whether what you will pay for the sponsorship and the cost and effort of promoting the sponsorship will be value for money.

The British Steel example.

Visibility varies between sponsorships. British Steel received good media coverage for its round-the-world yacht race, 'The British Steel Challenge', but to ensure adequate visibility, the sponsored yachts each needed to take the name of the sponsor. But how many members of the audience will have remembered the names of the individual yachts afterwards? However, if the audience consisted of business contacts interested in yachting, visibility may have been sufficient for the costs involved.

The Bristol & West example.

The Bristol & West Building Society chose bowls for its sponsorship, knowing that the activity appealed mainly to the retired and those approaching retirement, a market containing many potential investors. To maintain continuity throughout the year, the sponsorship was divided between indoor and outdoor bowls. Realising the game's potential for younger players, the sponsorship extended to a bowls league for schools. The next stage established a bowls tournament for disabled players including those in wheelchairs and the blind.

Although young people and the disabled can be potential customers, far more importantly the Society was seen as bringing something extra to the game. It was encouraging young people to take an interest and helping to ensure the game's long term appeal and survival. The Society was also demonstrating that its concerns were not solely with the more fortunate members of society. Such a broadminded approach gained extra goodwill, not least with the media and helped to raise the company's profile still further.

Many of the events were very good value particularly those that were televised. The game matched the Society's budget enabling it to be properly supported and promoted. The Society's audience was matched for its investment products. The treasurers of bowls clubs were also targeted with a special investment account intended for clubs and societies.

It makes sense that those interested in motor sport for example, are interested in motoring generally. This is an obvious sponsorship opportunity for the manufacturers of motor vehicles and accessories, fuels and lubricants, and for ferry operators. As caravanners are interested in touring, the same companies could sponsor events for these and at a lower cost than motor sport.

Given a large enough audience, a substantial number will be interested in such mainstream activities as golf, football, rugby and horse racing. Equally, if you have enough people for a niche event such as an organ recital, this would probably be as cost-effective as one of the high profile, high cost, activities. Research, and market feedback from those in daily contact with the target audience can help develop these activities.

A company that sees its business as being up-market will not sponsor a down-market activity. A company that sponsors show jumping certainly wouldn't sponsor snooker. This is an extreme example, but companies with mainly young customers do not sponsor events that appeal to the elderly. Similarly, companies with a family market do not sponsor something aimed at single people or childless couples.

Some sectors have to be discreet. Indications that substantial sums are being spent on promoting pharmaceuticals for example, could upset politicians and others lobbying on health grounds. It might also offend members of the medical profession. Even so, there is still scope for sponsoring activities of interest to general practitioners and others involved in specifying drugs. One major pharmaceutical manufacturer sponsored a newspaper for GPs. They made sure that the publication was not used solely to promote their products by including articles on leisure activities such as travel.

Not every business can derive the same benefit from a sponsorship. Many sponsored activities are aimed at people who are consumers whatever their interests. The essential element is that the sponsorship must encourage them to buy a company's products or use its services. It follows that companies with a strong consumer presence, either on the high street or from high profile products are more interested in sponsorship than other companies that are not in this position.

The link with the consumer.

Companies have different links with consumers. Banks, building societies and major retail chains, all have direct links with consumers. This is also true for insurance companies, the major public utilities, and the principal manufacturers of consumer products. Companies that manufacture components for motor vehicles will only have a consumer link if they also sell their products directly to the consumer under their own name. Companies that provide industrial process machinery, shopfitters, and the manufacturers of major capital goods such as aircraft and power station equipment, do not have the link with the consumer that would make sponsorship worthwhile.

There is a substantial element of marketing aimed at the 'business-to-business' market, and this can provide an opportunity for sponsorship. A wholesaler may sponsor something that raises his profile with local retailers and caterers for example. An office equipment manufacturer may want to entertain those who specify office equipment. Such companies will be more selective in what they sponsor and will look for an entertainment or hospitality opportunity rather than an activity aimed at the mass market.

TERRITORY

The geography of the market.

In a world where business is becoming increasingly international in scope, it might appear strange to place some emphasis on targeting the precise area in which a company is operating. Whether a company is operating on a global scale, across a continent, within one country, or simply a region within that country, sponsorship should match the geographical spread of activity if it is to have any impact at all. No impact means that money is being wasted.

If the sponsorship consists of a major national event, only companies that have a truly nationwide scope should provide support. The heavy costs involved confine such activities to companies with the resources to make use of the many publicity and corporate hospitality possibilities on offer.

Local sponsorships do not have to be reserved for local or regional businesses. Many businesses will do something for the population of their home town, or for their customers, employees, professional connections and other audiences. Major national companies should consider a local sponsorship if they can strengthen their presence and raise their profile in a major town or city. Artistic activities are most likely to benefit from such a policy, but it can also assist sporting events, especially in the location of the finals of a national competition.

The Bristol & West Building Society's sponsorship of bowls did not include crown green bowls because this is largely confined to the north of England where the Society had no branches and little business. Because it had branches in Scotland, bowls tournaments in Scotland were sought and sponsored.

The same applies to charitable donations. Most companies respond to demands for support by confining donations to those areas where they conduct business. This is a recognition that funds are limited and that it is better to be more generous within a precise area than to spread the money too thinly.

International sponsorships can be more difficult to find and promote. One of the best examples is the Olympic Games, but the costs are too high for a single sponsor. Various companies advertise themselves as the 'official supplier of...' or the 'official airline of...', but the only sponsor able to show a consistent sponsorship success is the manufacturer of the timing equipment, whose name appears when the elapsed time has to be shown.

Two solutions present themselves. The first, as with the Rugby World Cup, is to integrate television advertising or programme sponsorship with the sponsorship. Before and after events, and during any commercial breaks the name of the main sponsor is screened. The second is to liaise with the responsible bodies in the relevant countries and arrange a new international event that can be sponsored.

Both solutions have their drawbacks. Advertising and programme sponsorship adds heavily to the costs of the main sponsorship. Many believe that there are too many arranged events adding confusion and even exhaustion amongst athletes, not to mention the supporters! Global sponsorship can be expensive and is only justifiable for global brands, as the case study at the end of this chapter shows. Arranging tours by performing arts companies, or taking an art collection from one country to another, can both be used to establish international sponsorships providing that the event is correctly targeted.

For the smaller company in a localised area, a local team will always present a sponsorship opportunity. However, association with the team might be submerged by mentions of their success in a league sponsored by another, larger, company.

Companies sometimes sponsor a local activity that is visiting outside their normal business catchment area. They must be convinced that they will obtain sufficient benefit in their home town for their generosity.

THE DESIRED IMAGE OF THE COMPANY, ITS PRODUCTS OR BRANDS

Businesses vary, and many like to believe that they are distinctive in one way or another. Sometimes this takes the form of a particular emphasis in corporate identity or in advertising. Airlines and banks in particular need to foster a distinctive feel, judging by advertising that encourages consumers to 'fly the friendly skies' or deal with the 'bank that likes to say yes'. Possibly these arise because the product is not distinctive. Airlines use the same aircraft, with a choice of only two or three models available from the manufacturers for any particular type of route. Banks also offer the same products, with less chance to distinguish their products than motor vehicle manufacturers, for example.

Developing an image.

The choice of sponsorship or charitable support can change the image of the company. The need for a company perceived as being hard to look for a 'cuddly' sponsorship has already been mentioned. Such a sponsorship could be concerned with young children or young animals, for example. A company wishing to be perceived as go-ahead could opt for a sponsorship involving advanced technology, even sponsoring a competition for inventions by young people. If a motor vehicle manufacturer added four-wheel drive vehicles to its product range, added emphasis to the new range could be achieved by sponsoring show jumping or other pursuits with a rural interest. Oil companies have sponsored competitions for vehicles with low energy consumption, fostering the image of concern for the environment and the future.

Remember that companies succeed not through imitating their competitors, even though occasionally they need to introduce competing products simply to offer customers a broad range of products. In the case of sponsorship, the fact that a competitor does something is a case for doing something with an equal or higher profile, but not for doing the same thing! If one company sponsors a local football team, its main competitor should not agree to sponsor a rival football team. Whenever possible, good businessmen want alternatives, not to follow or confirm that a competitor has done the right thing by copying them. Worst of all, they do not want a rival's success on the games field to have other implications for the cynical observer!

CASE STUDY

Organisation: United Distillers

Background: The market for Scotch whisky has come under considerable pressure in recent years, partly due to younger customers being attracted to drinks with a less traditional image, and partly because of competition from Irish, American and Japanese brands.

Strategy: United Distillers has a large number of brands, but research showed that of these 'Johnnie Walker' was the one most associated with whisky drinking in the public mind. It also had the advantage of being a global brand as opposed to one targeted at a niche market. The research also showed a strong connection between whisky and Scotland, and between Scotland and golf. Golf also had the advantage of being a game with global appeal.

United Distillers commenced a global sponsorship of golf centred around the biennial Ryder Cup and using a distinctive 'Ryder Cup, Johnnie Walker' sponsorship branding. Supporting the Ryder Cup were other championships with nine qualifying events in Europe, eight in the United States, and seven elsewhere in the world including Japan and Australia. From these, players could progress to participation in the Ryder Cup. In years when the Ryder Cup contest was not being played, the company sponsored the Professional Golfers Association (PGA) competitions.

The sponsorship combined a global focus with targeted competitions in individual markets. The Johnnie Walker Classic, which counted as a qualifying event for the Ryder Cup, was played at different venues in Asia including Singapore and Phuket in Thailand. Competitors in each event came from the main countries in the region. To contribute further to the game, the sponsorship also extended to supporting amateur as well as professional players, and at the opposite extreme from the global focus included support at club level.

Result: Regular tracking surveys showed a growing appreciation of Johnnie Walker as the leading brand of Scotsh whisky and it benefited from its association with golf, a popular sport in most countries.

CHECKLIST

- Always be clear over the objectives of a sponsorship programme. Is it to improve the image, promote the product or brand, or is there some other objective?
- Can you readily identify the audience and will the sponsorship reach it?
- What activity or event is of most interest or concern to these audiences?
- Which geographical territories need to be covered in the sponsorship?
- What is the desired image of the company, its products or brands – traditional or go-ahead, town or country, young or old?
- Will the sponsorship clash with the efforts of a competitor?

Chapter 4

Responsibilities and Policies

The different arrangements that companies have for handling sponsorship and charitable donations often reflect substantial differences in the nature of the business and in corporate culture. There are only a few examples of companies that have applied some arbitrary rule in deciding which department or individual is responsible for these activities. They are normally found in smaller companies or professional practices that may have been forced to take other factors into account and give the responsibility to whoever appears to have the time or the inclination to take it over.

The different arrangements for handling sponsorship and charitable donations might appear strange to those accustomed to the order of many marketing departments. No one would ever suggest that advertising a company's products or its brands should belong anywhere other than marketing. So why should sponsorship sometimes be part of marketing, and sometimes part of public relations or corporate affairs? Why should charitable donations sometimes belong to the company secretary or the head of personnel?

Which department?

There are other ways in which these activities seem to defy the normal arrangements for controlling the activities of a major company. Advertising is usually controlled centrally, and companies with substantial branch networks are reluctant to encourage too much local advertising. This applies particularly to weekly local newspapers that are often far more expensive and sometimes less effective than advertising in the national media. By contrast, there is often a strong local link in both sponsorship and charitable donations.

The deciding factor for these arrangements should be that

arrangement which will work in the context of the company's needs and its organisation.

Companies that delegate charitable donations to personnel for example, believe that charity should have a human touch, and that it may also affect employee attitudes towards the organisation. These companies may encourage employees to take secondments with charities, or encourage charity fund-raising by their employees.

Sponsorship might belong to public relations or corporate affairs if the target audience consists of opinion formers, or if there is a substantial media relations aspect in the choice of activities to be sponsored. Some companies believe that everything related to the image of the organisation should be the responsibility of corporate affairs, and this will include charitable donations and sponsorship.

Local sponsorship and donations.

Many companies with a retail network feel compelled to support local needs and initiatives, particularly banks and building societies. How much delegated responsibility a branch manager can be given is an important question, and must be answered if local relationships are not to be impaired.

The division of activity must be understood throughout the organisation. Equally important is to arrive at a workable solution that meets local needs and the organisation's requirements. In short, workable solutions are more important than departmental grandeur.

There are three main steps to take:

1. Decide which department takes overall responsibility.
2. Establish a policy.
3. Establish a system that enables local and regional sponsorships and charitable donations to co-exist alongside national and, if necessary, international activity.

The question of which department should manage sponsorship and charitable donations appears to be of minor importance. Nevertheless, it cannot be avoided, especially in preparing a practical and efficient system at point 3.

WHOSE FUNCTION IS IT?

Sponsorship sometimes belongs to marketing, or as part of a public relations or corporate affairs function. Some businesses handle their own sponsorship, others use consultants or may have hybrid arrangements.

Charitable donations often belong to a corporate affairs function, but can belong to the company secretary's department or even to personnel.

There is some logic in these arrangements. If sponsorship is to promote the product and support sales or business development through corporate hospitality, marketing seems to be a fair choice. Image, name-awareness, community, political or investor relations, all suggest that public relations should have the responsibility. It can be argued that because sponsorship can be an alternative to advertising, marketing should make the decisions. On the other hand, because one major objective of many sponsorships must be to raise media coverage, then public relations seems to be the natural home.

Sponsorship could be divided between marketing, public relations, or corporate affairs, depending on the objective. If community relations are an essential part of the sponsorship objective, then charitable donations could belong to that function as well.

One has to be driven by the objectives in deciding exactly where sponsorship should lie. Close co-operation between marketing and public relations will be essential if sponsorship is to be integrated with advertising, and if media relations are to be successfully developed for the sponsorship. If one target audience is more important than the rest, then sponsorship should rest with the department responsible for the target audience. There would be duplication of effort and of skills if the bulk of sponsorship were handled by marketing, aimed at consumers or distributors, leaving public relations to manage a small rump of image-building sponsorship.

Whether sponsorship should be handled in-house or by consultants will depend on a number of factors. The most important is whether your company has the staff to handle the sponsorship. If the company is new to sponsorship the answer is probably no. The same may be true in a smaller company. A smaller company or a company with a relatively small marketing function is unlikely to have the spare capacity to handle the sponsorship. **In-house or consultants?**

Sponsorship consultancy support can be separated from event management. Many consultants offer both, but many client companies will handle one activity themselves and use the consultancy for the other. The question of looking for the right sponsorship, and for the right sponsorship consultant, is covered in Chapter 6.

ESTABLISHING A POLICY

Given the desire of directors and senior management to influence sponsorship policy and charitable donations, it is important that policies reflect the consensus among them.

Board level expenditure.

In many companies, the level of expenditure for a major sponsorship will require board approval, or at least the courtesy of notifying the board. Few companies will delegate authority for a high profile sponsorship costing millions over several years to middle management. The board will expect to be asked for overall approval. Responsibility for handling the sponsorship properly will be delegated to the individual charged with management and coordination of sponsorship. A strong board with non-executive directors who take their responsibilities seriously is a good counter to chairmen or chief executives who are fond of pressing for their favourite hobby as a vehicle for sponsorship.

A complementary policy.

A policy can be as difficult or as easy as one wishes to make it. A company solely sponsoring golf could complement this policy by concentrating charitable donations on professional golfers who have fallen on hard times. Alternatively, sponsorship could be devoted solely to angling. Charitable support could then be used for environmental projects concerned with the protection of rivers and other inland waterways, fighting pollution, and research into diseases affecting fish.

The other extreme is to have a sponsorship and charitable donations manual running to two or three volumes ensuring that every conceivable eventuality is covered.

One needs to be practical. The sponsorship and charitable donations policy should cover a number of points. It should allow everyone concerned with the subject to know exactly where they stand, not just for one year or even two years, but for the foreseeable future. The sponsorship and charitable donations policies do not have to be the same document. It is completely acceptable to operate both activities separately. One might miss some worthwhile opportunities in this way, but it might also make life much simpler.

Don't approach sponsorship with a pre-determined idea about what you would like your company to sponsor. Rather, have clear marketing objectives and an understanding of your audience, and then look for a sponsorship that will meet these aims.

The policy should embrace:

1. The extent of the delegated responsibility for making decisions. You should know how much authority you have, and understand when you have either to refer a proposition upwards or merely notify your superiors of your decision.

   You should also know how far upwards decisions have to be taken for any given size of sponsorship or charitable donation. Does it go to senior management or to the board, or, if there is one, a holding company?

   In many companies, the staff handling these matters will have a figure which they can operate within on a day-to-day basis, especially for donations. Their line manager or head of department will have a higher figure. Larger sums can be authorised by a committee possibly including one or two board directors, whereas the largest sums have to be approved by the board.

2. The objectives and target audiences for sponsorship.

3. Whether sponsorship is to be concentrated into one activity or more. Many companies like to have a major sports and a major arts sponsorship. Major companies or groups may have as many as six different areas of sponsorship and community involvement. Excessively fragmented activity means that the sums are spent too widely.

4. Other criteria such as company involvement in the locations where sponsorship is to take place; the need to have entertainment opportunities, or openings for staff or customers to become involved.

5. Expectations, which could mean only sponsoring activities that will receive television coverage for example, even though this could be very restricting. It might be that only sponsorships that include certain groups such as children will be considered.

6. Restrictions, such as refusing to sponsor activities that are

international, that do not provide opportunities for the disabled, or might be controversial because of animal welfare implications. Sporting events with crowd or team behaviour problems might not be supported.

7. Commitment, including setting a minimum period for major sponsorships, but always allowing sufficient flexibility for ad hoc sponsorship opportunities to augment the core programme.

8. Priorities, including preferences for supporting sponsorships or charitable activities in the area where head office is situated, or perhaps within a certain distance of factories.

9. Preferences, for a particular type of event, activity or charity.

10. It is also perfectly possible to nominate a target category of charity, such as those that work in the interests of young children or those favouring the elderly.

Publicising the policy.

The policy and the objectives should be widely available and understood so that your time and that of people requesting sponsorship is not wasted by requests being sent to head office. It is argued that revealing a sponsorship or charitable donations policy to the outside world might result in a flood of requests for support. The opposite is true in that revealing such a policy might discourage many unwanted requests. If it does encourage applications that fit into the policy guidelines, then there is the chance of being offered something attractive to the organisation.

DEVELOPING A SYSTEM FOR MANAGING SUPPORT

Sponsorships are often offered to, and charitable donations sought from, local management. The problem is acute for retail businesses with their high profile in shopping centres, but factories or other installations are major local employers and will attract attention as well.

The problem is compounded by two further difficulties. The first is that local management have little idea of what 'sponsorship' or 'charitable donation' mean, especially in the business sense. They are likely to make a donation to a local football club, expecting nothing in return and call this sponsorship.

The second problem is that many of those seeking support have little idea of what they are doing. Charity fund-raisers know that they want a charitable donation, but if you offer to take an advertisement in the local parish church magazine and call it sponsorship, no one will argue. Those seeking sponsorship genuinely do not understand that the sponsor has expectations that a worthwhile sponsorship must achieve. Fund-raisers believe that your company will support them because, in the words of one journalist, 'it is a nice thing to do'. As far as they are concerned, they are engaged in something worthwhile, such as running a local arts festival, flower show or football club, and so it deserves your company's help.

There are instances of organisers of events or activities obtaining sponsorship and then failing to do anything to assist the sponsor reap the benefits of the sponsorship, but these are rare. When organisers fail to deliver the results, the more likely explanations are ignorance and incompetence, rather than deceit.

It is possible to issue an edict that no local sponsorship can be considered, and that all charitable donations will be handled centrally. This would be unpopular and result in a number of problems, the first being that the company would be seen as mean. Local businessmen would discover this from their organisations such as Rotary or the Lions and business would start to drift towards a competitor. The second problem might be that local management would surreptitiously find ways of diverting some of its budget towards such activities.

Worst of all, some worthwhile opportunities might be missed. These could include opportunities to enhance the company's image through supporting local causes and develop additional business.

Selected local sponsorships can be used as an extension of national sponsorships further raising awareness.

It has to be accepted that approaches by fund-raisers to local management will be made, and can go wrong. The difficulty is that the line management for the local staff is unlikely to be through marketing, public relations or corporate affairs. This is inevitable and reinforces the need for board level approval of the policy and for the policy to be widely distributed, accepted and understood.

In devising any solution to this problem the senior line management responsible for locations away from head office will have to be involved. The ideal solution will vary from one company to another, and it might differ between sponsorship and charitable donations.

With sponsorship, the local management could be instructed to consider only those sponsorships that fit into the overall theme of the national sponsorships. Proposals must be referred to the coordinator of all sponsorship approvals. Strict guidelines must be laid down over mentions in programmes, on posters, and opportunities for posters to be positioned at the event announcing your company as the sponsor.

Prepare stock 'sponsor's statements' ready for inclusion in programmes with artwork for advertisements and logos.

Do not allow teams or individuals to be sponsored locally, not least because you could suddenly find two branches supporting opposing teams in a contest!

With charitable donations, allow local management to make individual donations up to a certain figure and establish an annual ceiling for all donations per branch. Regional management can have a higher figure. Do not allow donations to be made to local branches of national or international charities. This might result in certain charities receiving an unduly high level of support; instead insist on local charities.

A sponsorship opportunity might arise in a location that you want to support nationally; the same could apply to a charitable donation such as a major community project. Alternatively, a local sponsorship could be offered that would be difficult to refuse, but with little significant advantage to your company. In such cases, take the line of least resistance, offer a donation and ask to be listed as a sponsor, but forego the full list of demands and expectations of a sponsor.

One can do as much good in many local charity and sponsorship opportunities by offering a few golf umbrellas as prizes for a raffle as one can by applying stringent and costly rules.

Allow yourself the freedom to commit the company to sponsor an employee, another individual or group whose home is close to your company's head office. Torvill and Dean, the Olympic figure skating ex-champions, were supported by their local authority, but a business sponsor could well have benefited from their success.

A record should be kept of all sponsorship projects and their costs. This should also be done for charitable donations so that these can be included in the annual report. The charity can benefit from tax reclaimed on the donation effectively raising the value of your company's donation by a third on the tax rates prevalent at the time of writing.

CHECKLIST

- Find a department or an individual to take responsibility for sponsorship, settle on arrangements that will work and be practical rather than risking departmental infighting.
- Do the same for charitable donations. It might be a different department or individual, or it could be the same so that social sponsorship opportunities are not overlooked.
- Do not be afraid to recommend using a sponsorship consultant, especially if your company is new to sponsorship.
- Prepare a sponsorship and charitable donations policy that is acceptable to the board.
- Ensure that the policy is widely circulated and readily understood by management at all levels, and that other employees are aware of it.
- Ensure that local or regional management and those running subsidiary companies also have a role to play and are aware of it.

Chapter 5
Budgets and Planning

Budgeting and planning for sponsorship and, to a lesser extent, charitable donations, can be more complicated than for other marketing and public relations activities. The big difference is because you might be planning, and budgeting, for two or more years ahead. Given the amount of time and effort to be applied to a major sponsorship before it even starts, one can be working for at least a year before the first event takes place.

The complications that arise are those of inflation, for which forecasts are notoriously unreliable, and the prosperity of your company.

Promotional expenditure shouldn't be cut when business conditions are difficult. However, it is tempting to make cuts in this area when faced with the alternatives of cutting the number of employees, which can be expensive and will affect morale, or by deferring major capital expenditure.

In-built flexibility. Faced with such problems, you will have to allow a certain amount of flexibility. Your core sponsorship programme may be for two or more years, but each year this can be expanded or contracted. Minor sponsorships or complementary regional sponsorships can be added to the programme. If you sponsor opera, you can always sponsor a production at a regional centre over and above your existing programme.

Another means of gaining flexibility is by having sponsorships that are due for renewal at different times. If you have a core programme comprising three major sponsorships, perhaps sports, arts and community sponsorships, try to make sure that they are never due for renewal in the same year. Apart from the workload of handling three renewals simultaneously, you can decide either to renew only two of them, or opt for something less expensive.

In any case, renewal is not always automatic, and it does take time to evaluate an alternative sponsorship once you have decided that it is time for a change.

Breaking a sponsorship agreement, or even asking to be released from it, is something to be avoided at all costs. Substantial and costly financial penalties might be involved, possibly made worse by the time and costs of litigation. Worse still, the poor publicity will undermine any good that the sponsorship may have done. Other organisers of high quality events will be wary of working with you in the future. One factor that must be put to the Finance Director if he or she still insists, is that suspending or breaking a sponsorship agreement will send distress signals to the outside world and undermine customer and investor confidence in the company.

Don't break agreements.

The same holds true for any agreement to support a charity over a number of years. The charity might not insist on receiving its donations, but it is not unknown for this to happen, especially when covenants with substantial tax benefits have been in danger of being broken. The bad publicity revealing to the world at large that times are desperate, will do more damage to the company than anyone would wish.

You can always cut back on supporting expenditure or even on the quality of corporate hospitality. This will make the sponsorship less worthwhile, but at least the supporting items can be reinstated when business improves, and the corporate reputation will still be relatively untarnished.

You will want continuity in sponsorship, deriving the benefit of sponsoring over a reasonable period without sticking with one sponsorship for so long that the benefits have started to fall away. This amounts to an appreciation that sponsorship is a contractual arrangement, and both parties must see it in this light.

There is no consensus on what is a reasonable sum to allocate to sponsorship. There is no magic figure such as a certain percentage of turnover, or a ratio of sponsorship expenditure to advertising revenue. Although some companies like to allocate at least the equivalent of one per cent of distributed dividends to charitable donations, this is also discretionary. Such figures do not help those businesses that do not distribute dividends, such as building societies and mutual life offices.

Arriving at a figure.

It should be seen as fortunate that there is no fixed figure determining sponsorship expenditure. A decision on sponsorship will need to be taken in the light of other marketing programmes. Given your level of product or brand development and the prevailing market conditions, there will be a need to judge sponsorship opportunities against advertising or special offers, for example.

In assessing a reasonable sum to devote to sponsorship, start by considering the level of expenditure of your major competitors, or of companies in other sectors that have the same volume of turnover as yours. If you find such figures hard to obtain, sponsorship consultants can help in estimating the costs. These estimates will be fairly accurate as they will know whether a particular sponsorship has been offered around, or if one of their clients turned it down as being too expensive.

One can consider how much a particular type of sponsorship with a given profile will cost and use this as a benchmark. You can also take into account the level of support being given. The costs and the likely profile of a sponsorship can then be considered by setting it against your benchmark.

Costing consultants. The consultancy's own costs might be more difficult to assess. Sponsorship consultancies vary enormously in both the quality of their work and the fees charged, and it often seems that there is little relationship between cost and service. Some consultancies reduce their retainer and compensate by adding a substantial handling fee to their disbursement. Others prefer a higher consultancy fee and forward suppliers' invoices direct to the client for settlement without adding a charge of their own. Some charge the higher retainer and a handling fee!

Although the larger and more experienced sponsorship consultancies provide a full service, items can be isolated from the services on offer and the consultancy used for selected items. The main items include:

❑ Sponsorship consultancy, including advice and assistance with negotiations.
❑ Media relations, including press office management and a results service at events.
❑ Event management, relieving your company of the organisation of an individual event.

EVALUATING EXISTING SPONSORSHIPS AND CHARITABLE DONATIONS

In Chapter 6, we will consider the value of using research to gauge the effectiveness of sponsorship, especially when this is brand- or product-orientated. There is also a need to make decisions that go beyond this. Research will guide you on whether a particular sponsorship is worthwhile and cost-effective. It can also indicate which activities you should consider sponsoring by providing a profile for your audience and showing their main interests.

Research cannot make decisions for you. Finally, you have to take the initiative and the responsibility for proposing schemes that will work for your company.

You must start by looking at the existing sponsorship and charitable donations; are they working? Do they meet the specific requirements of the organisation in the case of sponsorship? For charitable donations, do you really know where the money goes?

Examine current arrangements.

You might find that substantial sums have been spent for years with little thought. There will be sponsorship that could be reduced to corporate hospitality exercises with a considerable saving or scrapped altogether with an even larger saving! There will be charities receiving small donations automatically for many years, while others perhaps more deserving will have been neglected.

What are the objectives of sponsorship in your company? Business, goodwill, image, community, investor or political relations? If anyone suggests that the answer is all of these, you may well find that the sponsored activity is serving none of these ends. The best sponsorship will have two or three objectives because it is almost impossible to find a sponsorship that does everything effectively.

You need to be assured that your organisation is receiving the right level of profile from its sponsorship in both quantity and quality. Although sponsorship works best over a period of three or four years, it is also possible for sponsorship to continue too long. Too short a term, and the connection with the sponsor fails to register with the audience; too long a term and the sponsorship merges into the background. There is also the risk in long-term sponsorships that the sponsor's support becomes taken for granted by those organising the event or activity.

Ask what the objectives of the sponsorship are, and using the list on page 24, decide whether it is appropriate for your organisation and its business.

Decisions must be made on the spread of resources for charitable donations. Are they to be distributed thinly but broadly or will they be concentrated? Will a few charities of each type be supported, or only those reflecting your organisation's business or location?

PLANNING

In Chapter 6, the problems of managing a sponsorship programme are examined in detail. Chapter 7 takes a similar approach to managing charitable donations. Before you get to the stage of managing a programme, you need to establish a policy over sponsorship as outlined in Chapter 4.

The essential elements in planning a major programme of sponsorship include:

❏ The objectives of the sponsorship, rather than any predetermined ideas on the sponsorship itself.
❏ Will the programme consist of one major sponsorship, or two sponsorships such as a major arts and a major sporting sponsorship, or three by adding community or social sponsorship?
❏ What will be the duration of any sponsorship? This should be at least two, or ideally three to four years with perhaps one renewal.
❏ In the case of two or more major sponsorships ensure that these overlap. This means that it could take up to four years to get a balanced sponsorship programme.
❏ What will be the timing of the events? Will they clash with major company events such as the announcement of financial results, which will prevent the public relations team and the directors from attending?
❏ Forthcoming changes to your company's board. Will a new chairman or chief executive feel the same way about sponsorships as those currently in office? It is wise to have a major sponsorship continuing for a year or so after such people have retired. However, anything that runs much longer could prove to be an irritant if the new team doesn't like it.

❏ Major expansion plans by your company. If a new product range or a new geographical expansion is planned, can the sponsorship programme be adjusted to cope?

❏ Possible contraction by the company will do the opposite, wasting much of your sponsorship programme that will probably have to be reduced.

This assumes that you will dispense with most of the minor sponsorships. This is a neat solution, but will not always be possible especially if you have to take local needs and objectives into account. Nevertheless, encourage local management to concentrate on sponsorships that are an extension of your core national or international sponsorships. This will provide greater benefit than undertaking something completely different.

Companies with an international spread of business may have to adapt their sponsorship strategy to take into account different national preferences. Ideally, look for sports, arts or community projects that are common to all territories, but if this is not possible look for something different. Football or tennis might be popular throughout Europe, but the same cannot be said about cricket unless your audience is solely the British expatriate community! Similarly, deep sea yacht racing does not have much of a following in Switzerland, Austria, Hungary, Slovakia or the Czech Republic.

National preferences.

One Anglo–French joint venture attempted to interest the British in the game of boules, without much success. The sponsorship was relatively inexpensive, but a waste of both money and opportunity.

Never underestimate the mood of your directors and their preferences. Life will be easier if it is possible to combine their enthusiasm with a clear business interest. At major events you want their support and presence. Producing a sponsorship programme they loathe could leave you with difficulties at a flagship event with VIP guests.

PREPARING A SPONSORSHIP BUDGET

You could decide that the sponsorship budget is simply a case of doubling the cost of the sponsorship deal, then dividing that among the various other items, such as entertainment and promotional items.

You can work in this way, but it would be better to plan to spend as much again supporting and promoting the sponsorship, but don't assume the right to do this.

In preparing a budget, you need to consider your company's philosophy. For example:

❏ Will the company charge out such items as office accommodation? If so, this overhead will have to be incorporated into the budget.
❏ If promotional items are to be provided, will the cost be charged to the sponsorship budget, or to local or divisional management according to use?
❏ Will the cost of tickets for guests be charged to local or divisional budgets, or met from your budget?
❏ Who bears other costs, such as the cost of lunches between senior management and the media; the cost of producing the advertising and posters; and photography to support the sponsorship?
❏ Can items of equipment be hired for as little as a day or two, or leased for a longer period? If they must be purchased, what is the practice for depreciation?
❏ Are there other costs that have to be allowed for, such as postage and electricity?

These are in addition to questions of the cost of the sponsorship itself, the supporting programme of activity, and the cost of sponsorship consultants and event management.

To charge or not to charge?

The practice of charging out to divisions or to local management has many adherents in business today. The theory is good, but in practice it can lead to serious problems, nowhere more so than in sponsorship. For example, if you attempt to charge a regional manager for the cost of taking his or her guests to a sponsored concert you will be told that the same seats can be obtained for a fraction of the price. Compromise by accepting the difference between sponsorship and corporate hospitality, provide the tickets free and leave local management to meet the costs of hospitality. You could reclaim the cost of tickets using standard box office prices, but the cost of administration might outweigh the relatively small sums recovered.

Of course, if the sponsorship is being used to support a single brand, life is much simpler. Charging out doesn't become a major factor.

Items that you might need to allow for include:

❏ The sums due to the organisers of the sponsored event.
❏ Additional sums negotiated such as personal appearances by stars.
❏ Cost of preparing a sponsorship branding, and whether this can be spread over two or more years.
❏ The retaining and any additional costs for a sponsorship or PR consultancy.
❏ Cost of preparing advertising and the negotiated cost of the media space.
❏ Cost of posters and the charges incurred in putting them up and taking them down again.
❏ The price of promotional items, and whether this can be spread over the period of the sponsorship.
❏ Corporate hospitality costs.
❏ The cost of any additional tickets that might need to be obtained.
❏ The cost of equipment for setting up a press office including telephone lines.
❏ The cost of your staff, and any additional or consultancy staff required.
❏ Overtime costs as many sponsored events run through into unsocial hours.
❏ Travel and subsistence costs for your staff and those of any consultancy.
❏ Whether you are charged for your own office space and other facilities.
❏ The cost of market research to assess the value and effectiveness of the sponsorship.

When assessing your own staff costs take into account any additional charges such as staff benefits, national insurance and pension contributions. Most companies have a standard procedure for this. You might also include the cost of a document outlining your sponsorship and charitable donations policy and achievements.

These are the basic points forming the structure of any budget before taking into account the workload itself. Without due attention to these items any budget is liable to be wrongly constructed in the first place.

For financial institutions and others that have to bear the cost of

VAT, it is important to remember that only the cost of printing is exempt from VAT – designers, video production companies and photographers will all be charging VAT.

In-house functions will find that their employing organisation will have its own policies and systems. Some companies budget for everything, some charge everything out to other departments, others see the time spent allocating and recovering costs as an unjustifiable additional cost in itself. The larger and more diverse the organisation, the more emphasis is placed on cost allocation and recovery. A cynic might suggest that this is why overhead costs rise disproportionately to the growth in size: an economist would describe this as the 'law of diminishing returns'.

The larger the organisation and the bigger the sponsorship, the more likely it is to be cost-effective. Big sponsorships are automatically big news because of the sums involved.

Inflationary pressures.

Major stumbling blocks when budgeting over a period are those items where costs are likely to fluctuate. This will happen if there is a wage settlement or an employee performance appraisal over the period of a budget, but it can also happen with other areas of the budget. The most common problem lies in estimating paper and printing costs. Apart from the impact of wage negotiations in the printing industry, paper costs are notoriously prone to fluctuations as a result of currency movements.

In most companies the finance director's team will have some longer-term inflation projections for use when considering major capital expenditure projects; these figures can be used for sponsorship. You could use the government's figures for inflation, but not all activities inflate at the same rate. Again, not all companies accept inflation as an inevitable built-in cost, and you will need to be assured of the policy before making any rash promises to the organisers.

Finally, you could consider adding in an incentive clause to encourage the organisers, with so much more if crowd attendance exceeds a certain figure, or if television viewing figures go beyond a certain point.

BUDGETING FOR CHARITABLE DONATIONS

Some companies do not budget for charitable donations, but assess every request on its merits awarding a sum according to the perceived need. This policy has something to be said for it, but it is wiser to gain approval for a fixed sum each year. It is also important to discover whether your directors will allow longer-term regular commitments.

Although you can add many of the costs shown in the sponsorship budget section to the cost of managing charitable donations, it is not acceptable to add these costs to the charitable donations. The figure declared to the Inland Revenue and shown in your company's annual report will be the sums disbursed.

Parent or holding companies must have an accurate return of all charitable donations made by subsidiaries for mention in the annual report.

The funds can be divided widely and sparsely, or major payments made to a small selection of charities. It is important to decide on the flow of funds over the year. You can have a major annual award and refuse everything for the rest of the year, but this is not the best way because you never know what deserving cause will emerge during the year. It is also good management to leave the company cash flow unaffected, and instead allow a measured amount to be distributed throughout the year.

The annual budget.

Fund-raisers are at their most active from January to June, and from September to the end of November. Requests for support are at their lowest in July, August and December. If your projected expenditure is broken down on a monthly or quarterly basis, give these three months much lower figures – perhaps half what you would donate in the other months.

CHECKLIST

- Objectives and target audience before pre-determined ideas.
- Use research to validate decisions.
- Take advice, using consultants whenever necessary and only dispensing with their services as in-house experience and capability grows.
- Be aware of the likely costs.
- Be familiar with your company's budgeting and charging policies.
- Keep projections for inflation up-to-date.

Chapter 6
Managing Sponsorship

Sponsorship should never be regarded in isolation. It is not merely added on to other promotional activity – it is an integral part of a marketing or community relations strategy. A lapse from this policy can only be permitted when the company adds an activity because it is important to its industry or its home town.

Managing requests.
It is possible to be constructive about those impositions suffered by companies because they are the largest employer in a town, or the major bank in a small country. The psychological blackmail in these sponsorships is concealing the fact that the organisers have tried everyone else. They may be treating the company in question as a last resort. Or the sponsorship is the last of a list of events the best of which have been taken by other sponsors. The answer is to use one's position, be aware of what is on offer, and make use of the sponsorship best suited to your overall programme.

Sponsorship can be part of programmes beyond marketing by including not just community relations but investor relations, political liaison and even media relations. This is not to suggest that marketing should ever ignore these other activities. Investors or other interested audiences can also become customers providing that the product is consumer orientated. On the other hand, it would be wrong to interfere to the extent that the main message was lost.

A sponsorship programme does not have to be confined to sports or to the arts; it can be spread over several different types of activity. It is not uncommon for large companies and groups to support five or six different areas of sponsorship. For smaller companies it is better to handle one sponsorship well than to spread resources too thinly over too many activities. Most companies will find that a sports and an arts sponsorship will be sufficient for their resources. If more is available a community or social sponsorship can be added, and perhaps have both a visual arts and a performing arts sponsorship.

In common with advertising, sponsorship is better as a continuing programme rather than a series of ad hoc exercises. It can take a year or two from the start of a sponsorship before a new sponsor starts to reap the full benefits. Just as an advertising programme can be boosted to make the most of opportunities or to provide additional support at key periods, the core sponsorship programme can often be augmented by minor, but related, sponsorships. The difference with advertising is that although one can cut back on advertising for a period, sponsorships need to be maintained. One will save little by cancelling sponsorship of a concert two weeks before the event, and lose considerable face and credibility.

A continuing programme.

Despite the other reasons for sponsorship, most sponsorship has customer loyalty, profile, and market share as its basis. Companies should take sponsorship into account when preparing a marketing strategy and a budget. The process has to be led by the company itself, or its marketing advisors. These essential strategic decisions cannot be left to the advertising agency. The most professional agencies may recommend sponsorship as part of the programme, but others will perceive sponsorship as taking a share of funds that should be devoted to creative work and media buying.

This proactive, company led, approach has to be taken even further. You do not wait for the organisers of events to approach you, and then take a decision. By the law of averages most of those seeking sponsorship will have little to offer, although there will be some attractive exceptions. A company with a clear cut and easily comprehended sponsorship policy will attract outside offers that should not be ignored.

Making the first approach.

Any company taking sponsorship seriously as an integral part of its marketing plan must identify relevant events or activities and make the first approach when necessary.

SEEKING THE RIGHT EVENT

Bearing in mind the opportunities offered by sponsorship listed on pages 25–30 in Chapter 2, the objectives for the sponsorship must be clear. It is permissible to have more than one objective as long as you have an agreed set of priorities. Is image more important than entertaining customers? Are you more concerned with retaining the loyalty of existing customers, or is the objective to find new customers?

If image is important, what type of image does your company want? It is not enough to suggest a wider appreciation of the new corporate identity, instead you must consider such concepts as 'caring', 'progressive', or even 'traditional'. You will find more direct marketing objectives easier to justify and to attain.

The next step is to identify the right sponsorship, one that is compatible with your business and with the profile of the audience. You may need to have researched your target audience to learn more about the profile and their interests. One early problem might be that the best sponsorship opportunities are already taken. It is conceivable that the programme will take some time to develop before suitable alternatives can be found, or created.

Useful organisations.

Fortunately, help is available. In the United Kingdom, the Institute of Sports Sponsorship (ISS) and the Association for Business Sponsorship of the Arts (ABSA) exist to bring commercial sponsors together with sport or the arts. ABSA in particular is able to devise campaigns tailored to suit the needs of the prospective sponsor, and maintains links with sponsors after sponsorship programmes have been established. There is also an annual award for the best arts sponsorship – which looks good and will sound even better on your CV!

SPONSORSHIP CONSULTANCY

The European Sponsorship Consultants Association (ESCA) is another useful source of advice and assistance. ESCA can help the prospective sponsor identify objectives and prepare a brief. Guidance is then provided on which of its members would be most suitable given the category of sponsorship and the geographical location.

Selecting a consultancy.

You can ask two or more consultancies to pitch for your business. However, the relatively small number of consultancies means that this is less common than it is with advertising agencies or with public relations consultancies. Arts sponsorship consultancy in particular is seldom awarded as a result of pitching.

An alternative means of selecting a consultancy is to arrange a few informal discussions with the organisers of major sponsorship events, and with journalists accustomed to covering such events to find out which seems to work best.

In finding the right consultancy, and eventually the right sponsorship, you must prepare a thorough briefing. If the briefing document is weak or superficial, the results are likely to be unsatisfactory. If you are short of essential information about your markets and your target audience, a good consultancy will offer to research this information for you. It would be well to take their advice, otherwise a great deal of time, effort and money could be wasted on the wrong sponsorship. Worse still, you might find that you are committed for several years.

Whether the consultancy handles the negotiations on your behalf or merely advises, the brief will be important. Its preparation may well clarify many of your own thoughts.

You must be clear about the services you expect from the consultancy. Negotiations, preparation, events organisation, media relations, advertising, and sponsorship branding are all services that will be on offer. Some of these may already exist in-house, or you may wish your usual advertising agency to handle any advertising arising out of the sponsorship to ensure compatibility. Many major sponsors handle most or all of the work themselves, but such companies have the resources and the experience to do so.

Clarity over your expectations from the sponsorship will be important, not only for the consultant, but also to concentrate your thoughts and ensure that there is a consensus amongst the management team. Is peak period television coverage essential? Alternatively, your target audience might take little interest in television programmes.

It is easy to make too much of a problem out of this early stage in sponsorship, but careful attention to detail now will pay rewards later.

PITFALLS TO BE AVOIDED

There are a number of traps for the unwary or inexperienced. The need for the sponsorship to become widely known should mean that companies confine their sponsorship to those territories where there is significant business, or a good prospect of creating a significant business. There is no point in a company whose business is purely UK-based sponsoring a ballet in Moscow. Similarly, an American company with no plans to enter the European market should not provide support for the Royal Ballet in London, or even for an American ballet or orchestra to tour Europe.

Avoiding controversy.

Businesses wish to avoid controversy as far as possible because they can become embroiled in controversy in their normal course of business. The following should be avoided: sports with a bad reputation for crowd violence or unsporting behaviour by the participants; events held at poor quality grounds; poor theatres or other venues; artistic companies with a poor reputation; and temperamental performers who might miss an engagement.

Only the naive or the brave will allow their employers or clients to be exposed to such difficulties. Even the brave and optimistic will do so only with a full recognition of the problems and with a plan for improving the situation.

You should beware of taking caution too far. Sponsoring a notoriously dangerous sport would be foolhardy, but many sports have some element of risk. Providing this is put into perspective the sponsor's image should not be tarnished by the occasional accident.

Not sponsoring individuals.

Wise business people are also wary of sponsoring individuals who can easily fall from grace, suffer an accident, or simply fail to win. Companies using major show business or sporting personalities in their television advertising pay substantial insurance premiums to protect themselves against the death or injury of the star. This is a little more difficult in the case of a sponsored individual and is an unwelcome additional cost for budgets that are never quite big enough.

These reasons also discourage many companies from sponsoring teams, preferring to sponsor events. Teams can be unsuccessful and many companies do not wish to be associated with failure.

Excluding individuals or teams from the sponsorship programme might be unnecessarily restrictive for major companies who might wish to adopt such a course. Smaller localised businesses may find that such a sponsorship receives acclaim in their neighbourhood, helps employees to identify with the company, and is within the more limited budget. Even larger companies might wish to sponsor an employee selected to represent his or her country in an amateur sport.

There is no easy or inexpensive way of stopping two or three rival companies using the same event for corporate hospitality. However, in the case of outright sponsorship, the sponsoring company should ensure that no competitor is allowed to advertise at the event or in the programme. At an event with a principal sponsor allowing smaller sponsors for parts of the event, you can try to ensure that competitors of the principal sponsor are not allowed to take part. The term 'competitor' can be widely interpreted – a bank will not allow building societies as well as other banks to take part.

Dealing with rivals.

The only occasion when these basic rules can be rejected by the organisers of an event are those cases in which the restrictions would be too severe. It would be difficult and controversial to attempt to insist on such rules at the Ideal Home Exhibition or the Royal Smithfield Show, for example.

Finally, if the right opportunity doesn't arise, don't waste funds on unsuitable activities. You can always increase other aspects of your budget to achieve the same objectives. The main reason for not sponsoring is that the sponsorship programme will not produce the anticipated results, and you will lose the support of your directors and senior management for sponsorship. There is also the danger that committing your company to an unsatisfactory sponsorship might mean that you do not have the resources to take advantage of the right opportunity when it arises. A cynic might suggest that you will also be regarded as naive and an easy target for the organisers of events which are decidedly second rate.

When not to sponsor.

THE VITAL STEPS

It is possible to express the arrangement of a sponsorship in a series of steps:

1. Establish clear and precise objectives for the sponsorship.
2. Be sure that you know your market and your audience.
3. Be aware of your competitors and their sponsorships, to avoid clashing.

4. Prepare a brief for the sponsorship consultant if you feel that your company needs this support.
5. Identify a suitable consultancy if one is needed.
6. Consider what is likely to be suitable, bearing in mind the matching process mentioned in Chapter 3.
7. Find out what is available, and when, since the ideal sponsorship might have a year or two left with an existing sponsor.
8. If nothing suitable is available within a reasonable timescale, look for activities that can be developed.
9. Establish a preliminary contact with the organisers of events or activities that appear to be suitable.
10. If the initial discussions are encouraging, start to prepare the programme or campaign.

SCHEDULING THE SPONSORSHIP

Many companies enjoy direct contact with the organisers of the events being sponsored, even if a sponsorship consultancy is retained. You should not leave everything to the consultants, and you cannot avoid being involved because any agreement will be between your company and the organisers.

Timing is important. Depending on the size of the sponsorship, you will need time to prepare. In the case of a really substantial sponsorship, a year or two might be necessary for all of the preparations to be put in hand.

Responsible sponsors usually provide the organisers of the sponsored event with at least a year's notice that they will not be renewing the sponsorship, and this gives you an idea of the timescale. This is not only honourable, allowing the organisers time in which to find a new sponsor, but it also recognises the time required to establish a new sponsorship from scratch.

As mentioned in Chapter 5, if you have several major sponsorships, try to ensure that these have different renewal dates, providing your company with flexibility and not placing an undue strain on resources.

NEGOTIATING A SPONSORSHIP AGREEMENT

Sponsors and the sponsored must be partners in a deal that provides both with considerable tangible benefits. You should never be pessimistic over a potential sponsorship that proves difficult at the negotiating stage, or where the organisers seem concerned about what may seem to be the finer points of detail. Pedantry might irritate at the time, but it is far better to have tough negotiations than to spend the duration of the sponsorship embroiled in arguments or renegotiation. The better understood both positions are at the outset, the easier it will be for both parties once the sponsorship commences.

First, there must be a sponsorship agreement that is clearly acceptable to both parties. This will allow for any flexibility required including, for example, a formula for dealing with inflation. Goodwill is necessary, but the initial euphoria should not result in an agreement that lacks detail and ultimately leads to a breakdown in relations. You may even find that a simple exchange of letters will be sufficient, especially for smaller sponsorships. Remember that the best deals are between a willing vendor and a willing purchaser.

Sponsorship is a partnership.

If you do leave the negotiations to a sponsorship consultant, it is essential that their brief and the extent of their authority is clear. No one can negotiate effectively if their objectives are in doubt, neither will negotiations work if you countermand or refuse to support matters that have been agreed between the consultants and the organisers.

Get it absolutely right at the beginning, and never lose sight of your objectives for the sponsorship. Be absolutely certain about your reasons. Establish what it is you are promoting: the organisation itself, an operating division or subsidiary, or a product or a brand.

You will need to know that the sponsorship:

❏ can reach the right audience, or audiences;
❏ that there will be no risk of conflict with corporate objectives and no chance of embarrassment – appreciating that certain activities might be controversial, have a risk factor due to safety or other considerations, and might not be appropriate in image terms;
❏ meets your marketing objectives and either has an obvious link with your business or its customers, or that such a link can be forged;
❏ costs have been correctly identified and accurately estimated;
❏ is being run by people who are capable and reliable organisers;

❏ is being run by people able and willing to obtain publicity within their specialised media and with specialised journalists in the general media, who may be different from the usual media contacts known to your PR department or usual consultancy;

❏ will not be announced to the outside world without the text of this, and any other major announcements regarding the sponsorship, being agreed with your own press office or PR consultancy;

❏ will not be shared because this creates confusion and divided loyalties among those being sponsored, and effectively reduces media coverage as journalists, short on time, space and patience, cannot be expected to mention every sponsor;

❏ offers the opportunity, whenever possible, for your organisation's name to be linked with that of the event, and if this is not possible, all publicity material should mention the sponsor;

❏ leaves you with sufficient funds available to incorporate the sponsorship into advertising and to produce promotional items and entertainment possibilities relevant to the sponsorship;

❏ includes some form of added value, so that sportsmen or famous entertainers can meet your company's guests at a social occasion after a game or a performance, adding considerably to the sense of occasion for the guests;

❏ can be accompanied by research to show awareness of your company's, or brand's name amongst the target audience before and after the sponsorship (unless it is an ad hoc event);

❏ should not usually include teams or individuals, who might be involved in controversy or even suffer illness, death or injury, preventing them from fulfilling the sponsorship;

❏ if it is a major sponsorship, it can be maintained for two or more years, so that the benefit of being associated with a particular activity is enhanced by repeat exposure, just as advertising often goes unnoticed at first and needs repeat exposure; but

❏ is not going to be maintained for so long that the sponsor's name is likely to become taken for granted, merging into the background;

❏ if it is an ad hoc sponsorship, that it fits with your core sponsorship, or at least one of them as major companies may have as many as five or six areas of sponsorship at any one time.

If the list sounds demanding it is because your company will be committing a substantial amount of money and effort into what could be a major business proposition. The possibility of controversy, the need to be able to explain the company's objectives, and the media interest in the cost of the sponsorship, all mean that media relations will always be important. Chapter 8 deals with this in depth. Nevertheless, the organisers of the event or activity will need to be able to speak freely about their own sport or other event, and one must be careful not to impose censorship.

A prospective sponsor would be wise to visit the venues for major **Venue and facilities.** events when this is appropriate. They must be suitable for the activity and for any additional plans such as entertaining and advertising. If the venue is used for many different events, will there be time for the sponsors of other events to have their material removed and your banners, posters and advertisements put up?

The sponsorship agreement must cover many of the items listed here. It must specify exactly those facilities and services that your company expects, and the duration of the sponsorship. If extra money is likely to be required during the term of the agreement, annual inflationary or review clauses should be inserted. If elements such as television coverage are in doubt, it is possible to specify a certain sum for no television coverage, with a higher sum if this occurs.

COMMUNICATING A SPONSORSHIP

Chapter 8 looks at media relations for both sponsorships and charitable donations in greater detail, and the question of managing a sponsorship and the need to devolve authority was covered in Chapter 4.

There is another important need, which is to ensure that everyone inside your company is aware of the sponsorship and the reasons for it.

Mention of a substantial sponsorship and the sums involved can **Publicising the cost.** sometimes produce an adverse reaction amongst staff, including senior managers. Usually, the cost of even a major sponsorship amounts to far less than a company's annual expenditure on advertising, but advertising budgets do not have the same impact in the general media as a major sponsorship. The cost of a sponsorship will almost invariably be announced, partly because this contributes to its newsworthiness, also to the profile of the sponsor. Even if figures are withheld, many in the industry will have a shrewd idea of a likely figure and estimates will abound. Fortunately, the 'cost' of a sponsorship is simply that of the sponsorship alone; the many additional items of expenditure that need to be included in your budget are seldom taken into account.

Staff benefits.

Sponsorships that include benefits for staff or their families, such as reduced rate admission, are often viewed in a better light than those that seem completely remote from employees. If staff realise that prospective and existing customers will be entertained at the sponsored event, they will appreciate the benefits to the business and, ultimately, to their own job security.

Staff should be told about new sponsorships as soon as these are announced, perhaps circulating a copy of the press release as a circular or notice board item. Follow-up in the employee newspaper or magazine, and on any employee communications video news programme, will also help to keep them involved. Rather than simply repeating the original announcement, such follow-up coverage can include interviews with the sponsorship or marketing manager, explaining why the sponsorship has been chosen and what is expected from it.

Corporate hospitality.

If there are to be opportunities for corporate entertaining, members of management in a position to invite guests should be left in no doubt about the objectives, and that means ensuring that they invite the right kind of guests. Especially in a long running sponsorship, the sponsor will often find that the same guests appear again and again. These will be friends of a branch manager for example, rather than the sponsorship being promoted through their customers and potential customers.

The ideal way of maximising the benefits of corporate hospitality is to invite managers to nominate guests, specifying exactly what constitutes the ideal guest. 'Nominate' is the key word here, they should not be allowed to invite guests on their own. Once their lists have been approved, it might be a nice touch to allow individual managers to provide their own guests with tickets. If there is any doubt about their ability to handle this matter, tickets and other material should be distributed centrally. There is a great deal of routine administration to conducting a successful sponsorship, as the checklist at the end of this chapter will show.

Case Studies

Organisation: Lloyds Bank

Objectives: To use sponsorship to raise and improve the Bank's profile with young people, the potential customers of tomorrow. Lloyds wished to be viewed as being modern, friendly and accessible, and believed that by attracting customers while they are young, they are unlikely to move their business elsewhere in later years.

Background: Competition among banks and building societies for the business of young people remains intense in many countries, including Great Britain. People seldom move their accounts from one bank to another, so any bank that can attract customers early in life can expect to retain their business. As the smallest of the four largest British banks, Lloyds has been a less convenient bank to use in many areas than its larger competitors. Nevertheless, it is viewed as a bank for the more affluent and wished to attract young customers who fitted this profile.

Strategy: The common theme decided for all Lloyds bank sponsorship activity was to be quality, youth, their aspirations and education. Three elements were decided on:

❑ The Lloyds Bank Theatre Challenge. This offered schools the possibility of entering a nationwide competition to discover the most talented and original drama group. There were local and regional heats leading to a national final. In addition to the prize, the project offered schools professional evaluation of their school plays by experienced actors and theatrical producers. The best were performed at the National Theatre in London. Leading actors and actresses were patrons of the challenge giving it additional credibility with schools.
❑ The Lloyds Bank Fashion Challenge. A nationwide competition in which young people between eleven and eighteen years old had to design an outfit for a named celebrity. A series of local heats led to a national competition. The regional winners had their designs made into finished garments and modelled by professional models in a televised fashion show. The competition attracted entries from more than 15,000 schools. The final was broadcast by BBC Television's programme 'The Clothes Show' and was watched by 9 million viewers. The winning entries were also shown at the 'Clothes Show Live Exhibition', which Lloyds Bank sponsored at the National Exhibition Centre in Birmingham.
❑ The British Broadcasting Corporation's annual musical event for young people, the 'BBC Young Musician of the Year', was sponsored by Lloyds Bank. The programme was watched by almost twenty million viewers, many of them in the higher and more affluent social classes, who constituted an important target audience for Lloyds Bank.

These sponsorships blended to show Lloyds Bank as caring and interested in young people, as well as stimulating creativity and supporting programmes that complement education. In addition to the guaranteed coverage of the Fashion Challenge and the Young Musician of the Year on national television, all three competitions ensured additional coverage on regional television and radio, as well as local, regional and national newspapers. They also provided an opportunity for bank branches to make contact with local schools and groups for young people. The local and regional competitions were notified to the local and regional newspapers who were provided with stories and photographs of the winners, especially those from a particular town in a newspaper's circulation area.

Results: Research showed that more than 80 per cent of the young people participating view Lloyds Bank as being modern, friendly and approachable, and the sort of bank they would choose. The young people involved were among the most intelligent, able, and often from affluent families. They were likely to be among the most ambitious and successful, offering the prospect of being not just additional customers for Lloyds Bank, but good customers. Obtaining impressive results from such sponsorship nevertheless requires tact. Companies that over-commercialise such activities risk losing the benefits of such sponsorship; in many countries there is resentment at any attempt to manipulate children for commercial gain.

Organisation: Nescafé

Objectives: Young people were found to be drinking less coffee, and Nescafé was concerned that the rising age profile of its customers would mean a fall in the demand for coffee in future years. Nescafé wished to increase coffee drinking among younger people, making them feel that it was a modern, exciting drink.

Background: In many countries, there is intense competition for the hot drinks market between tea, coffee and other drinks, and between the wide variety of brands on offer from competing producers.

Strategy: Nescafé decided to use sponsorship of a broadcast programme intended for young people. The company made use of this new sponsorship opportunity, which has been permitted in many countries for a number of years, but which is a relatively new opportunity in Great Britain. Rather than adopt an existing programme, Nescafé spent a year working with Capital Radio, one of the London local radio stations, and the Independent Broadcasting Authority (IBA) to develop a new programme that could be transmitted throughout the independent local radio network in Great Britain. The programme was a popular music programme, which each week transmitted the best-selling pop music records in Great Britain. The title eventually agreed was 'The Network Chart Show, brought to you by the Independent Radio Network and Nescafé'.

Most sponsorship messages need to be seen as well as heard, and Nescafé supported the radio sponsorship with a number of other promotional campaigns. These included the Nescafé Roadshow, a travelling disco featuring new pop groups, as well as becoming involved with local promotions with radio stations throughout Great Britain. Promotional merchandise such as T-shirts were produced and sold, and advertising taken in popular teenage magazines.

The additional activity recognised that sponsorship often needs to be supported extensively by other promotional activity, including advertising and merchandise. Often the supporting promotional activity can cost as much as the basic sponsorship. This is particularly so in the Nescafé case for, unlike the competitions run by Lloyds Bank, the radio programme lacked news value, being purely entertainment rather than educational.

Results: Research showed that more than 70 per cent of the target age group was aware of Nescafé's sponsorship and that their perception of Nescafé had improved.

CHECKLIST

- Allow yourself and your organisation enough time to find the right sponsorship, negotiate a sensible agreement, and have enough time for the preparations for the sponsorship.
- Allow a sufficiently large budget for the sponsorship to be supported by hospitality, promotional items or 'giveaways', and advertising.
- Do not forget how long it takes to select and prepare promotional items, or produce and print material to accompany the sponsorship.
- Ensure that communications are coordinated with the organisers of the event.
- Circulate details of the sponsorship and its objectives internally, especially to those who will be involved in nominating guests and acting as hosts.

- Establish clear rules for any hospitality exercises.
- Nominations for the guest list should be monitored centrally, and be with the sponsorship manager at least six weeks before the event.
- Have a reserve list of those who can be invited once the early refusals have been received, but try not to issue any invitations less than two weeks before the event to avoid causing offence.
- Invitations can only be issued once the nominations have been agreed.
- For events requiring tickets, only issue these once the invitations have been accepted; issuing these with invitations only encourages the passing on of tickets to others, completely undermining the object of the exercise.
- If customers generally are to be invited to attend an event, or if discounted tickets or vouchers are on offer, ensure that those handling the gate keep a record of these, both to avoid any argument over any money due and to monitor the popularity of the event with customers.
- If you are inviting customers en masse, do be clear what is on offer. Discounted tickets for a major agricultural show for example, might not necessarily extend to the right to join the chairman for sherry in a hospitality stand.
- Have adequate numbers of well-briefed staff available to handle nominations, invitations, the issue of tickets and the arrangement of seating plans for lunches or dinners.
- Have other staff ready to attend the venue before the day and install any equipment, posters and advertising material. Be sure whether or not any help can be provided by the organisers or those managing the venue.
- At the event, have staff ready to hand out promotional items – there are many cheap and cheerful promotional items such as hats and badges that will do much to raise the profile. Keep the more expensive golf umbrellas for the guests.
- Guests should be met by staff ready to provide guidance; these should be people prepared to work lengthy hours and still remain cheerful. Such staff must be briefed beforehand and given a tour of the venue.
- Never expect guests to behave rationally, at least once they become part of a group. Once part of a crowd, they will be difficult to move from one venue to another, even more difficult to separate from the bar! Have staff strategically positioned to make sure that guests don't get lost.
- Apart from signing your sponsorship and the entrance to the bar, make sure that cloakrooms and other essential locations are clearly signposted.
- Have a system for sweeping up lost property, and for passing on customer enquiries!

Chapter 7

Managing Charitable Donations

In most companies today, charitable donations are the responsibility of one of three departments: corporate affairs; the company secretary's; or personnel. However, the growth in social sponsorship and the importance of good customer relations mean that marketing is often involved as well. Liaison between marketing and the department that holds the charitable donations budget can be beneficial to the organisation and to the charity.

Donating money to worthy causes requires integrity on the part of the donor, including efficient record-keeping, not least for tax reasons. Administration must not become too heavy a burden or companies will find charitable donations too expensive.

The recent growth in sponsorship opportunities has been paralleled by the expansion in the number of charities, and in the opportunities for providing assistance. It is estimated that 99 per cent of companies make donations to charities. The problem is that relatively few have a policy – most are reactive, simply responding to charities who ask. Most donations are more than simple 'conscience money', and are made with the best of intentions, but there are instances where a donation is made simply to avoid embarrassing directors or members of the senior management team.

Requests to company staff.

You have to accept that directors and senior managers may be co-opted onto the committee of a charity and will be targeted by their peers at social events. Even local managers can find themselves in this position because to local people they *are the company*, regardless of whether head office regards them as holding senior positions.

If an important local customer approaches a local manager looking for a charitable donation, the manager may feel that a refusal might offend. The customer is probably too sensible to take offence and is simply asking everyone they meet.

Such activities could be seen as threats to budgets and good corporate housekeeping, but one should try to see them as opportunities. Organisations with a branch network or with factories in a number of locations, will often find that a great deal of goodwill can be generated by making suitable charitable donations. This can sometimes involve employees or customers as well.

Traditionally, those companies that give corporate donations to charities have been divided into those who contribute generously to a specific charitable cause, and those that spread their largesse thinly. The first approach is suited to companies with a particular and relatively narrow spread of business – the shipowner that concentrated on maritime charities, for example. Not all companies find establishing a policy so easy, and the second approach occurs when companies have a wide community involvement making it difficult to focus on a single charity or category of charities. These companies tend to spread their funds thinly, with the exception of one or two major appeals. An example of this approach was a major bank, which didn't have a budget for charitable donations, but accepted or rejected requests for donations and set the budget retrospectively at the total given over the year.

A policy of thick or thin?

A growing body of opinion among corporate donors believes that making a substantial number of small donations each year has little impact and increases administration costs both for the donors and for the charities.

Spreading donations thinly over a wide number of charities does increase the administrative costs of charitable giving, although the author does not know of a single company which adds this cost publicly to its charitable donations budget. Many donors take the view that a donation of £250 will be less than, for example, the proceeds of a flag day, and less than the amount many school or church-related charities will raise in a jumble or bring-and-buy sale.

Many charity workers argue against this approach, pointing out that the public are most likely to give to charities connected with animals or children. The public will also support fund-raising events for a hospital extension or the restoration of a much loved church.

The public is, however, far less inclined to support the elderly and the less well known diseases and ailments. For these, less obviously popular charities, small sums from a large number of businesses can add up to the necessary level of funding.

If you go along with this argument and if you are going to have to support local management, a facility for disbursing these small donations will be necessary. Sparing the embarrassment of your superiors will also require donations which may be small, but not that small.

There is no point in asking why managers and directors who are approached for a charitable donation do not reach into their own pockets. They are approached not as individuals but because of their position with their employer. The funds expected are on a corporate scale, and would be beyond the inclinations of many individuals. Those who do habitually provide generous support for charities have personal preferences about what they should support.

Few businesses respond to appeals by individuals, but there is scope for local companies to support appeals to assist worthy causes in their neighbourhood. Large companies also find it worthwhile in terms of employee relations and goodwill to assist an appeal for an employee or a close relative of an employee.

Generally, people seeking support for their education, or for what appears to be a holiday abroad (yes, such appeals are made), or for a student party, should be given a firm 'no'.

TARGETING DONATIONS

The first important step in deciding how, and whether, donations should be targeted is to have a policy decision on whether the company is interested in supporting charities, and if so, how it should provide such support. This decision should be made at board level.

As 99 per cent of companies provide charitable donations, it is likely that your company will wish to do the same. You need to know which of the following options have the approval of the board:

❏ Concentrating on charities which are specific to your geographical or business area, such as maritime charities for shipowners, rural charities for companies producing fertilisers, and so on.

❏ Supporting charities which are local to your company's head office, or the town in which the company was first founded.

❏ Selecting a small number of charities, perhaps one in each of the main fields, such as child welfare, medical research, and so on, and concentrating support on these.

❏ Spreading support more widely, but also more thinly in each case.

❏ Attempting to establish a combination of the two above, and if so, how.

❏ Deciding whether personnel can be seconded to work for charities for a period.

❏ Deciding to undertake social or community sponsorship, usually through an increase in the funds available for charitable donations and possibly by using part of the sponsorship budget for this purpose.

❏ Making a decision on how far charitable donations can be delegated to local level.

❏ Agreeing a budget for at least one year in advance, and deciding whether or not a budget can be set for the longer term so that projects lasting two or more years can be considered and given assurances of support.

If social sponsorship is the preferred course, an abrupt transfer of funds from charitable donations to social sponsorship will not be welcomed by those charities unable to offer sponsorship opportunities. A sudden change might have a negative effect on the company's image in the community and staff morale might be undermined. A decision to undertake a programme of social sponsorship should be accompanied by additional funding. If the sponsorship includes projects that are attractive and beneficial to the organisation some funds could be transferred from the sponsorship budget.

Social sponsorship programmes.

Many companies will go further than this. The supermarket chain, Sainsbury, launched a trust with initial funding of £200 million. The Royal Bank of Scotland established its Group Community Fund to support projects which benefit the environment, heritage and job creation. This is in addition to its charitable donations. Few of the projects handled by either of these could be regarded as social sponsorship, however.

Many companies have a sponsorship policy and it is also sensible to have a charities policy. Many companies have a well-produced document that describes their activities in the community. This can be used to gain credit for their efforts, and to encourage suitable requests for support and discourage those which are unsuitable.

All these measures are the result of high level policy decisions which show the commitment of companies' board directors. Those handling charitable donations can propose a policy and implement it, but the board must make decisions about fundamental aspects of it.

There is more scope for managers below board level to take decisions on other aspects of charitable support.

Support in kind.

Most companies will happily allow their management team to decide whether charities can receive support in kind. This might mean agreeing that the in-house printing operation prints leaflets and posters for the charity. The company's own transport might be available to deliver or collect goods for the charity, or premises might be made available for a charity function or press conference.

Obsolete office equipment has a poor resale value, so companies often donate old word processors and office furniture to charities. Companies like to use the latest equipment, furniture reflects the corporate image, and standardisation often has a high priority. Charities are not nearly so fussy, and your old word processor might be a significant improvement on their existing equipment.

If you decide to donate obsolete office equipment and furniture, do make sure that it belongs to the company. Some office equipment, especially photocopiers, will only be leased.

Many charities operate on a small scale, unable to obtain the benefits of bulk purchases, so simply by adding a few items to your order for furniture or word processors you might enable a charity to make a substantial saving.

Some newspapers will allow charities free space for an appeal advertisement and a television company may give free air time for appeals. Scottish Television's 'Box 2000' goes further, providing a camera crew and director so that charities can appeal for volunteers or make their assistance more widely known. Direct appeals for funds are not allowed. Occasionally transport operators will provide free advertising space on the poster sites at their termini, or indeed, on buses and suburban trains.

To keep the charity advertising within sensible and affordable limits media owners may select a particular space and position as 'the charity spot'. It might be necessary to insist on qualifying criteria to ensure fairness – local charities only and a strict rotation of the charities using the spot, for example.

There is an employee relations aspect to this, which can take many forms:

❑ Encouraging payroll-giving by donations deducted from the monthly salaries of employees. The amount plus the tax paid by the employee is available for donations to charities.

❑ Collecting boxes for major flag days, notably the annual Royal British Legion Poppy Appeal, can be made available at strategic points throughout business premises, usually at reception areas and canteens. You can have permanent collecting boxes but the impact will be lost if the customer sees more than one or two boxes on display at any one location.

Banks and building societies will often accept donations at the counter. These will be paid directly into a central account at no cost to the charity. Generally, when providing a donation collection service for charitable appeals, banks and building societies provide the same service regardless of whether or not the appeal is for a crisis in the UK or overseas.

❑ Encourage participation in those appeals which provide an outlet for the competitive energies of employees, whether it is a marathon or a sponsored bed race. These encourage team spirit and boost morale. As a bonus, they provide good 'copy' for the company newspaper. They might also get favourable coverage in the local press.

❑ The company may go further and agree to match donations raised by its employees at work. Obviously no company would dare offer to match the private donations of its employees! In 1992, National Westminster Bank spent £140,000 in this way.

Few companies would put pressure on their customers to support a charity. But there are more positive ways of encouraging participation including:

❑ The company could agree to make a donation to charity for each item purchased or for so much money being spent. The most obvious example of this is the so-called 'affinity card', in effect a credit card the use of which provides funds for a specific charity.

❏ One retail chain, Savacentre, made donations to charities close to each store when customers used their own bags rather than the free Savacentre carrier bags. Some Sainsbury's branches gave customers a small refund for each of their own bags used, and placed a charity collection box by the door in the hope that the small change refunded will go straight into the box. In each case, charities were assisted and there was an environmental benefit because fewer carrier bags were used.

❏ Another retail chain offered discounts in return for a donation to charity at the check out desk. This approach can cause an adverse reaction with some customers.

Media events such as 'Red Nose Day', 'Children in Need' and 'Telethon', encourage the public to raise money for charity. Many employees use this as another opportunity for joint fund-raising events.

Involving customers.   It is possible to involve customers as well, but care should be taken. One airline found that the crew of one of its aircraft was refusing to allow passengers to disembark unless they made a donation first. Putting customers on the spot in this way is embarrassing and thoughtless – neither you nor your colleagues have any idea of the individual's means and commitments, or of the extent to which any individual might already be supporting a charity.

One can sometimes encourage employees and customers to work together for charity. This approach works well in public houses and appeals to the competitive instinct of the regulars.

Funding a project.   Some corporate donors provide funding for specific projects or special appeals only. Others support the general work and overall funding of a charity. Some provide support for one year only, others provide support over a period of years.

It is not unusual for corporate donors to refuse to provide support for fund-raising itself. This can be difficult as many people believe that charities should earmark between 10 and 15 per cent of their estimated donations for fund-raising. Much depends on the acknowledgement that might be accorded to the business providing what is, in a sense, a degree of sponsorship or pump-priming.

Many companies are reluctant to provide donations for charities that operate outside their home country. This is not meanness but a sensible attempt to establish a policy. No one company can help everyone and everything and there are usually more than enough pressing local and national needs to keep those handling donations fully occupied.

Charities and territory.

Other companies respond only to charities which operate in those areas where the company has business interests even if this means two or more countries. In this way, local goodwill is maintained, and the company can be seen to be putting something back into the community in which it operates.

Charitable donations do not always reflect the generosity and kindliness of the proprietors. Many companies with fairly harsh attitudes give generously to a charitable appeal, especially if they realise that their image is a trifle dusty, and a well-publicised and generous donation to a local charity might impress local opinion.

New arrivals in an area, and especially those from overseas, may also see the provision of charitable donations as a means of showing that they will be good neighbours and making an early good impression.

Most companies provide charitable support without demanding public recognition, but it is silly to ignore the media opportunities that can arise if a large donation is being made. The main national media are only interested in stories which involve at least tens of millions, but local and regional newspapers will be interested in smaller sums, especially if the charity is local.

Public recognition.

One has to consider the market. A story which arises in London needs to be big, but smaller donations will be newsworthy in Cardiff, Belfast or Edinburgh. The same applies in Europe. The major French national newspapers are as difficult to get coverage in as their British counterparts. Belgium and the Netherlands, being smaller countries, will often cover stories where the donation has a smaller price tag. In Germany and Spain, there are strong regional newspapers which, if professionally targeted, will assess news on a regional basis rather than applying national criteria.

ASSESSING CHARITIES

Charitable activity varies widely, and so does the appeal of individual charities. People may or may not have sympathy with a certain disadvantaged group or a particular cause. This is one reason why charities exist – they give us the opportunity to support those causes dearest to us, or which arouse concern. This is better than leaving everything to the state.

Of course, when one is not making decisions for oneself, but for one's employer, more objective criteria need to be followed.

National councils.

Help and advice in assessing charities is available. The National Council for Voluntary Organisations (NCVO) or in Scotland, the Scottish Council for Voluntary Organisations, can provide advice and guidance in making donations to charities. You can also check with the Charity Commission in England and Wales, or the Inland Revenue in Scotland, to discover whether or not a particular charity is registered. While this is no firm guarantee that everything is as it should be, because of the sheer number of charities which have to be monitored by the Charity Commission, it will eliminate some of the worst offenders.

Not all of the organisations you wish to help will be registered as a charity. If your company is offered the opportunity of having a suitable period advertisement on a restored bus or railway station, or its livery on a restored commercial vehicle, it is unlikely that such a project would have charitable status. This would have to be seen as sponsorship.

A railway or canal restoration project might be supported if your donations policy includes heritage projects, but these may not have charitable status.

One also has to bear in mind the organisation's attitude towards political donations, since some charities have a distinctly political flavour.

The questions to be asked.

It is difficult, even impossible, to judge between many different needs. The average individual handling charitable donations is usually intelligent, diligent and humane. But does one support an appeal in this town or that town? Who is more deserving, the blind or the deaf, those with mobility problems, the mentally handicapped, or orphans? You cannot carry your own preferences into the workplace unless you own the business.

Essentially, you either target charities which your organisation feels justify considerable support, probably no more than about ten or twelve, or you have to assess each request for support. There is no reason why the entire budget can't be devoted to a single charity. Certain charities are so well-known that they are beyond reproach and these will receive support. But what about the rest? There are a number of simple steps to help you decide which to support:

❏ Eliminate charities that fall outside your company's policy on donations.

❏ Discover whether the charity is registered with the Charity Commissioners in England and Wales, or the Inland Revenue in Scotland.

❏ Who will benefit from funding? Look at the beneficiaries and the other sources of help available to them. If a substantial donation is requested, a copy of the charity's annual report will show how much goes into their work and how much is spent on administration.

❏ If the request is for an advertisement in the programme for an event, or an offer of tickets for a charity dinner, consider carefully whether or not the charity will receive a worthwhile share of the money. Offer a donation instead, at a figure about 25 per cent of that sought for the advertisement or for the tickets.

❏ Avoid charities which might clash with your business. Some church-based charities have clashed with banks and bankers, for example, often using ill-conceived arguments. Would you wish to support a charity that attacks your company?

❏ Avoid appeals for an individual, unless there is a link with your company or its home town as these are notoriously difficult to assess fairly.

❏ Consider whether the appeal is one which lends itself to social sponsorship, to staff or even customer involvement.

These basic rules will help. But if you are working for a company of any size with a significant presence in the community many will turn to it for help. Occasionally, especially in the less densely-populated parts of Britain and Europe, a single substantial business will feel morally obliged to act as a fairy godmother to the local community.

Sometimes it is possible to involve a charity in one of your own events. One building society had the delightful practice of commissioning new cash machines, or ATMs, by inviting a local celebrity to

Relating charity with your business.

make the first withdrawal. The sum withdrawn was donated to the charity of their choice. This practice, and that of providing a donation when new branches opened, spread to other building societies and banks. Sadly, cash machines are introduced less frequently than was once the case, and new branches are even rarer!

The Royal Bank of Scotland capitalised on its role as a note issuer by having a locally important person cut through a ribbon that incorporated a bank note when opening new premises. The picture of a note being cut had strong media appeal and the 'LIP' was allowed to donate £100 to his or her favourite charity.

INVOLVING STAFF

The idea of involving staff is good but has to be monitored and controlled. Staff enthusiasm must not be allowed to risk souring customer relations. Companies won't want staff to bring the business into disrepute. It might be fun (and shows a warm corporate sense of humour) for staff to wear red noses for Comic Relief day; anything too boisterous in the workplace may upset customers or cause an accident. The questions to ask are: is the company prepared to match the money raised by staff, and will company time be given to staff involved in a charitable appeal?

Informing staff.   The important factor is that staff should understand that the company has a charitable donations programme, and what is the policy. This has two advantages. The first is staff will realise that the company has a human side to it and takes its place in the community seriously. This can have a beneficial impact on morale and on the corporate culture. The second is that managers of branches or other locations will be clear about what they can agree to, what ideas might be entertained favourably by head office, and which are likely to be rejected. Clear policies avoid difficulties and embarrassment and informed local managers will help to reduce unnecessary requests for support.

Whether the company matches staff fund-raising pound for pound will depend both on the economic climate and on the other charitable commitments of the company.

Releasing staff time.   Allowing staff time off might mean organising a secondment, or allowing staff who have been helping with a flag day to come into the office later – once the rush hour crowd has disappeared from the streets and local bus or railway stations. If office staff can help in this way it benefits charities collecting in areas dominated by office and industrial premises. Charities have little difficulty in persuading supporters who are not working, and those who have retired, to collect in their local shopping centre. But big industrial estates and large areas dominated by offices, such as the City of London and parts of central Birmingham and Manchester, are more difficult. Whether staff can be released depends on whether or not they are handling work that can wait half-an-hour or an hour, or whether, as in the case of staff in retail premises, they will be missed by the customers, who will be inconvenienced.

Secondments are sometimes presented as offering managers a career development opportunity in a different environment. In many cases, the staff seconded are those who can easily be replaced but are not quite bad enough to be dismissed. There are two more worthwhile possibilities.

Do not second staff full-time, but allow a certain number of staff to work for a charity, partly in their own time but with the company matching the time they give, or a proportion of it. The rationale is that allowing someone a day per week in a different environment for a year or two might broaden their outlook and experience, without them losing interest and involvement in their career and their employer's needs.

The other possibility is to use secondment as a means of reducing early retirements or management redundancies, or even as part of a programme to prepare long-serving managers for retirement and outside interests.

Finally, never coerce, but instead wait for enthusiastic volunteers to step forward.

WORKING WITH CHARITIES

It is not always necessary to prepare an agreement when making a charitable donation. A simple letter committing the company to providing support and, when necessary, a covenant, will suffice. If the relationship develops into sponsorship, then of course the many requirements listed in the previous chapter could apply, depending on the extent of the relationship.

If you are funding a particular project, such as the provision of a facility at a hospital or the restoration of a room in a building, it is up to your company whether or not it wants a small plaque mentioning the sponsorship. Companies providing major educational benefits, such as a university chair, will usually expect to have their name incorporated in it, as the Glaxo case history shows.

Just as you would expect to agree the text of any press release concerning your company's support with the organisers of a sponsorship, you should expect the same from your support for a charity. But be realistic in your expectations as only major support really counts with the media. Remember too, that the media is not being unduly intrusive if it asks about the extent of your company's support for a charity, since the value is the measure of its newsworthiness.

Case studies:

Organisation: Glaxo Holdings

Background: Glaxo is one of the world's leading manufacturers of pharmaceutical products. It is a founder-member of the UK's Per Cent Club and in 1992 gave £8 million in the UK, equivalent to 5.2 per cent of the Group's total pre-tax UK profits. Given its extensive international interests, Glaxo also makes donations towards projects elsewhere in the world.

Policy: The policy is controlled by a Group Appeals Committee which gives priority to improving healthcare and promoting scientific and medical education. It also funds initiatives improving the environment and promoting good healthcare in the developing countries. A variety of performing and visual arts projects in the UK and overseas are also funded.
   The six main areas are:

1. Healthcare, helping the health services extend the quality and range of treatments, and providing new facilities in parts of the UK close to Glaxo's main operational centres. The programme extends to endowment of a chair in ophthalmic epidemiology at Moorfields Eye Hospital in London, and to a study of eye disease in the developing countries by the World Health Organisation.
2. Education, including the endowment of academic posts such as the Glaxo Professor of Molecular Parasitology at Cambridge, and help for facilities at universities and teaching hospitals.
3. International healthcare throughout the world working through both British-based international charities, such as the Cheshire Homes and the British Emergency Aid for Russia and the Republics, and locally-based charities.
4. Environmental projects, including those concerned with research and conservation.
5. The arts, through sponsorship of exhibitions, performances and by commissioning works of art from contemporary artists for Glaxo's own premises. Glaxo's business links with Japan were celebrated with a touring exhibition of Japanese porcelain.
6. Community projects throughout the world, including support for skills training and job creation. In Italy, Glaxo has introduced a 'Sport and health' programme to tackle social problems amongst young people in Verona, where the company has its Italian headquarters.

Organisation: British Telecom

Background: British Telecom donates in excess of £14 million annually to charities, having committed itself to donating half of its UK pre-tax profits to charity. The sum is equal to 60p per year per UK customer, and cannot be regarded as an imposition on the customers.

Policy: Since requests for such a high profile company far exceed the sums available, BT organises its donations into well-defined areas through a Community Programme. Most of the projects are linked with registered charities, while inner-city social projects to help those in need are often directed through the main churches.

There are six main areas:

1. The disabled. Giving grants for sporting and outdoor projects, and for those ensuring easier access. There are also awards for achievement.
2. Those in need. Helping major social themes such as homelessness, medical research, addiction to alcohol or drugs, and caring for dependants.
3. Economic regeneration, improving inner city areas and providing employment training and advice for new businesses. There is also a capital venture fund for expanding enterprises.
4. Education, providing up-to-date information on telecommunications for school courses, and providing communications services for schools, as well as teacher training and running a BT Museum.
5. Environment, with schemes to improve the UK environment and promote responsible practices.
6. Arts, with sponsorship bringing leading performers and companies, and exhibitions, to the widest possible audience in all parts of the UK.

CHECKLIST

- Your company must decide whether it is content to spread funds widely, or target specific areas of need more generously.
- Any policy must be flexible enough to allow for local initiatives and peer pressure on directors or senior management.
- If in doubt, check the credibility of charities, either through the Charity Commission or by inspection of their annual reports.
- Consider a policy document on charitable donations and sponsorship, highlighting your company's policies, its successful support of community initiatives, and highlighting those areas in which it intends to be involved.
- Support employee involvement in helping charities and in fund-raising.
- Be aware of sponsorship opportunities arising from charitable donations.
- Consider other means of supporting charities, including the offer of surplus equipment.

Chapter 8
Media Relations

Improved media relations is one important reason behind much sponsorship and some charitable donations. Sponsors will hope their name or that of their brand will be mentioned in media coverage of the event. This is one reason why incorporating the name of the company or the brand into that of the sponsorship is so important. Broadcast coverage usually guarantees two mentions of the sponsor's name, but not all newspaper journalists are so cooperative. Even those who won't mention that the event was sponsored by 'Doggy Chocs' find great difficulty in concealing this fact from their readers if the event is named 'The Doggy Chocs International Dog Sleigh Marathon'.

This does, however, raise two problems which you will need to keep in mind. The first stems from the fact that the public relations department or PR consultancy will know a lot about your business and the relevant media. They will know the journalists who write or broadcast about your business and the company's financial performance. The problem is they will be much less familiar with the sponsored activity.

The attempt to ensure that the sponsorship is compatible with the business will help to overcome this problem. Sponsoring motor racing or a caravan rally may be a sensible sponsorship for a ferry operator, but the public relations department will know far more about, and be more interested in ships.

Sponsoring a concert on the eve of announcing your company's annual results, and inviting investment analysts and fund managers as company guests, is fine, but how many people do you have who are knowledgeable about classical music?

Size of the press office. The second problem is that a worthwhile sponsorship with a high level of media interest, can place the press office under considerable extra pressure. The team will be staffed according to your normal business requirements – the company's financial reporting and industrial and community relations requirements – with a margin for crisis management.

Not that you should immediately hire a PR consultancy, extra staff, or ask your sponsorship consultant to take over. Any or a combination of these options might be necessary, but involve the press office management first. Apart from courtesy, coordination is important, and the sponsorship cannot be treated in isolation from other company activities.

Involve the press office when you start to consider a sponsorship. They are then able to deal with any media enquiries arising before the sponsorship starts. They can advise on the media possibilities of different sponsorships, and assess the commitment they will have to make. If it does place them under heavy pressure, they can also cooperate with you in devising a workable solution.

If the media discover that you are a potential sponsor, infamous rejoinders such as 'no comment' will confirm any rumour they are following. Although you will want secrecy and discretion, the organisers of the event may want early publicity. Their interests lie in committing you to the sponsorship as early and as publicly as possible to swing negotiations in their favour. Alternatively, they might raise the interest of a prospective rival sponsor, or encourage an existing sponsor to continue to provide support.

Media support means news, features and photographs rather than advertising. The difference is that you pay for advertising space or air time and have complete control over the message. With editorial you have little control because the message passes through the hands of a journalist. But the space or air time is free and is more likely to be noticed, not least because of the impartiality of the journalist.

There is a tendency to view the media as a threat rather than an opportunity. But good contact with the media, and a willingness to respond to their demands can be rewarding. Establishing contact gives you the opportunity to tell your story, advance your cause and heighten awareness. Journalists vary between those who can be trusted and those who cannot, but most realise that some adherence to a code of ethics will pay off in the longer term.

Good media contacts.

Major charitable donations can also generate good media relations. Charities can help by using their local networks of spokespeople. Charitable donations will place less pressure on the press office than sponsorship.

Media training.   There are few short-cuts in media training, but one method that is better than most and good value for money is the set of training videos *A Guide to Handling the Media* produced by BBS Productions in Bristol. This consists of three videos, one dealing with the press, another with radio interviews and the third with television interviews – the hardest and most effective medium. The videos are an introduction to the subject rather than a substitute for media training. If time or money is limited they are helpful and clearly outline the role of the media and the main pitfalls to be avoided.

Good media relations are important in any sponsorship. The larger the sums devoted to the sponsorship and the higher the profile of the event, the easier it is to attract media attention. Important events that are household names are newsworthy, so are large amounts of money. This is not to say that good media relations for a major sponsorship are easy. The planning and coordination will be more demanding because the risks of adverse media comment if anything goes wrong will be more serious. Those with lower profile and smaller budget sponsorships will have to work harder to attract the attention of the media and be more thoughtful about how they do this.

Once the sponsorship is operating, sponsors can expect the organisers of the event to handle media relations. This ability must be checked because some sporting and artistic bodies, especially the smaller or newer, may be unable to cope. Questions about the sponsorship itself should be answered by the sponsor, although the sponsor and the sponsored should always agree a joint line on every issue.

You should expect the organisers of the sponsored event to know and be known by those journalists most interested in their activity. The author well remembers a former employer taking over sponsorship of a major event, and finding that the sponsor would have to establish a press office, which had been unheard of by the organisers.

MEDIA RELATIONS FOR SPONSORSHIP

The main steps in handling media relations for sponsorship include:

1. Announcing the sponsorship and using cost as the yardstick of news value. Ensure that specialised journalists are not overlooked in the sponsor's desire to draw it to the attention of their own specialised press.
2. Individual events need publicising; there is also the need to provide facilities for journalists covering the event. With a sporting event this may extend to the provision of a press office. In addition to desks and chairs, this should contain typewriters, telephones, power points for portable word processors, a photocopier and tea and coffee facilities.

    Major artistic events such as exhibitions require previews. Drama productions must allow the press to attend a dress rehearsal or the first night, although the latter is of little use if the production is for only a few nights and the only newspaper available is the local weekly. Single events, such as a concert, operate on a review basis.
3. Negotiating with broadcasting stations for coverage, raising the sponsorship value of the event for the sponsor. The BBC is in a better position to arrange national coverage than ITV, which works through regional companies who take some nationally networked material but often confine themselves to providing regional coverage.

    Broadcast coverage of sponsored events usually includes a mention of the sponsor at the beginning of the broadcast and two mentions during the commentary. Someone will have to find adequate power points for a television crew. Banners and posters will be provided by the sponsors, but these must be positioned so that the television teams do not object.
4. There will also have to be supporting media activity including background information and photographs of competitors, athletes, teams and performers. Events such as training or rehearsals can also provide media opportunities.

Little of the above applies if the branch manager of a local retail outlet has just contributed £100 towards your local amateur dramatic society. A mention in the programme might be worthwhile, but a rave headline in the local newspaper shouldn't be expected. The so-called sponsorship is merely buying a limited measure of customer goodwill and little more. The requirements that you will have for a sponsorship must extend to more substantial events than this.

It is possible to adjust the event to improve media coverage. The sponsorship appeal of a major sporting event can be improved by major regional heats or finals to raise the profile of the event in the regions and provide additional opportunities for media exposure.

MEDIA RELATIONS FOR CHARITABLE DONATIONS

Many companies do not expect publicity or recognition for their charitable activities. Small donations particularly are not newsworthy – if every company donating £500 sent a press release to the newspapers in the charity's locality and those close to the company's head office, there would be an informal, but effective, ban on these offerings.

There will be major charitable donations that are worthy of a photograph of your chairman handing over a cheque to the chairman of the charity. If the sum is large enough, or the photograph can be interesting enough, at least local newspaper coverage is likely.

Charities will co-operate.

Charities will be happy to co-operate with major donors in gaining media coverage. There are two reasons for this – the first is that it pays to appease the donor. The second is that it helps the charity to be seen to be supported by businesses in the hope of encouraging others to follow.

Social and community sponsorship schemes will depend on publicity, and can be treated as being much like any other sponsorship.

The one essential rule in dealing with charities is that the charity should not announce your company's support to the media without clearing the press release with your press office or PR consultancy. You should, however, let the charity know when you are announcing your support to the media as a matter of courtesy.

Your press release should give a few details about the work of the charity. Even such well known charities as Guide Dogs for the Blind and the Royal National Lifeboat Institution need a few brief words of description. The number of people helped each year can be highlighted, for example. If your company is providing a replacement lifeboat, the number of launches made each year from its lifeboat station would help put the support into perspective. A new item of equipment for a hospital or research establishment can also be described in terms of the problem it will solve.

Although the costs of some sponsorship programmes, or 'deals', are not revealed, there is little justification for not revealing the amount of a charitable donation. Your annual report does not have to break down the amounts given to individual charities, but an overall figure is required. There is no reason for concealing this information and doing so will arouse suspicions.

NEWS

The news value of a sponsorship or a charitable appeal can be exaggerated by those whose proximity to the story causes them to lose their objectivity. It is not an overstatement that objectivity is the essential precondition for a good news sense.

Over-estimating the news value is an understandable human reaction, especially for those who have laboured long and hard on a project close to their hearts. However, the opposite happens with many good stories that are not fully appreciated by those involved. Modesty, or fear of having someone pick fault with a speech, can result in a news opportunity being missed. Many underestimate the impact of a particular project or development through failing to understand the interest of the outside world.

Judging the news value.

News value varies, and is hard to quantify; that is why so many PR people are former journalists. They use that instinctive or intuitive judgement about the impact of a story, and know which publications or broadcasting stations will be interested. Something that is useless for the national press could have considerable local or regional impact.

There is no automatic right to news coverage. News must have an impact, and an editor of a publication or news bulletin must be convinced that it is of sufficient interest to a reasonable proportion of the audience. Charities need to appeal to the general reader, but donors and sponsors need to consider specialised publications, or the arts or sporting pages of the general press. A story that is not worth the front page in the daily newspapers may receive excellent coverage

Where the story should appear.

on the sports pages, for example. If a sponsor decides that soccer supporters are the audience, then there is no problem with coverage in the sports pages.

If your story is local, don't waste time on the national or regional press. Don't pester the news editor if the story is better suited to the sports or the arts editors.

The usual method of getting news to the media is through a press release. The basic rules for drafting a press release include:

1. It must be brief, with no unnecessary words, superlatives or such pointless phrases as 'announces' or 'is pleased to announce'. Never state the obvious.

2. Leave adequate space at the top for the newspaper sub-editor to write instructions to the printer and to add his own headline – two inches should be sufficient. Leave a one-and-a-half inch left margin for editorial amendments and any additional instructions. Never type single spacing, use double spacing.

3. Put the date at the top – so that the news editor know whether the story is still current.

4. Look for a short, factual, eye-catching headline. The duty news editor will be 'sniffing' fifty or sixty stories a minute and may be short of newspaper space or broadcasting time. You have to work hard to ensure that your story is the one that will arrest his attention.

5. The main facts of the story should be included in the first paragraph. If space is short or the newspaper is about to be printed, this can be used on its own and give the reader all he or she needs to know.

6. Any quotes must be attributed to a director or other senior executive for credibility.

7. Keep each paragraph short with no more than three sentences. In the case of the first paragraph, one or two will do. It has to be easily read and understood, most newspaper paragraphs are kept very short, even in quality newspapers. If background or technical information is necessary, either prepare a separate press release for the technical media or add a supporting document.

8. A brief concluding statement about your company's business or the reputation of the brand can be helpful.

9. End the release with the name and telephone number of a contact. Include an out-of-office-hours number because many journalists work outside normal office hours. This should be typed after the end of the release – itself clearly marked by 'ENDS' to avoid confusion – and never printed as part of the press release paper in case the individuals concerned are absent on leave.

10. If the story is worth a good photograph, make sure that one is provided with a usable caption attached to the back. If a brochure, price list, or sample of the product would be useful, this should be added.

There is more to media coverage than news; features coverage should not be overlooked, nor the value of a good photograph.

FEATURES

Features have two purposes. The first is to inform by providing background to the news or bring the reader up-to-date on a development of interest. The other is to entertain. Sometimes a feature can do both – the regular theatre, opera, ballet and music reviews are good examples.

It is difficult to make news out of a well-established event. But news can be followed up over a period by features on the progress of a charity, major sporting or artistic event. A good feature can show how funds donated to a charity are being used and heighten awareness of the work being undertaken.

PHOTOGRAPHS

The old adage about a picture being worth a thousand words is more than a cliché, and it is worth considering the relevance of photographs to press releases and features.

Not every subject lends itself to a photograph, which itself must **What to photograph.** tell a story with little additional explanation. No one wants to see office workers or street collectors in their newspaper, but they may be interested in a photograph of a charity relief worker in the field. A sports personality in action will be interesting, but no one will be anxious to see a group photograph of the organising committee other than the committee members themselves.

Stage productions could use photographs of a dramatic scene taken during rehearsals. Perhaps something novel such as members of a concert orchestra struggling off the aeroplane with their instruments. Frivolous perhaps, but don't take yourself too seriously if you want to catch the eye of the picture editor. Campaigns by charities can find expression in photographs – starving children, injured animals, the elderly are very powerful subjects for the photographer.

The role of the photograph in the news media has to be understood. All newspapers and magazines use photographs, but do not maintain vast armies of photographers. A London-based daily newspaper might have fewer than half-a-dozen photographers, and will depend heavily on material provided by news agencies. Photographs issued by charities or sponsored events organisers will be used if the standard is high enough and the photograph is fresh and newsworthy.

Black and white is best.

There is a technical as well as a creative aspect to the type of photograph newspapers or magazines will want. Newspapers and magazines print many of their photographs in black and white. Colour photographs printed in monochrome lack definition and contrast, producing a fuzzy or muddy result – good monochrome photography will provide a better result. To allow the editorial staff to reduce the photograph and retain quality, prints should be 8 inches by 6 inches, portrait photographs can be as small as 5 inches by 4 inches.

Colour prints reproduce less well in colour than colour transparencies. Colour transparencies should be at least $2\frac{1}{4}$ inches square, larger if a whole page or cover illustration is to be the end result.

Never ever assume that newspaper photographers will turn up no matter how important the event. Always invite them to major events but ensure that your own photographer is available. The Wright brothers' first aeroplane flights were ignored by the press despite their excellent reputation as glider pioneers. However, thanks to their foresight the photographs exist of that memorable day.

CONTACT WITH THE MEDIA

There is a balance to achieve in media relations. Courting the media unnecessarily risks disaster if taken too far, especially in the pro-motion of an individual. Ignoring the media or hiding from them risks being overlooked, or becoming suspect in their eyes.

Journalists get topics right more often than they get them wrong, but they cannot be expected to bore their readers, listeners or viewers with unnecessary detail.

Journalists who can speak to those with first hand knowledge produce a better and more accurate story than those who have to scrape around for information from whatever source might be available.

The wise organiser, or the directors and senior management of a significant sponsor or donor, will be readily accessible to the media. They will also aim to be sufficiently well respected by the media to have due regard given to their opinions. Good media ability at the highest level does not eliminate the need for professional PR advisers. The advisers should be monitoring contacts and sitting in on inter-views thereby improving their knowledge and their ability to act as a spokesman whenever the directors are absent.

Using advisers.

An approachable organisation will have reviewed its policies on the disclosure of information. It will have decided which of its management team will talk to the media and the limits of their authority. This is another reason why the professional PR adviser is so important.

The interests of the media and the organisation are not necessarily the same. Never waste the time of journalists; they may be working on a number of stories at the same time. A journalist could have invi-tations to half-a-dozen press conferences or receptions on any one day, most of these arranged for late morning or lunchtime. Journalists do not appreciate being invited to a press conference when a tele-phone call or even a simple press release would do.

Press conferences are only suitable for significant stories. The conference ensures that a consistent message is given to the media, who also have the opportunity of asking questions of the directors or senior management. Answers given at a press conference are more consistent than if a dozen journalists were to telephone and ask questions individually. Although journalists do not like sharing questions and answers with their rivals, they appreciate that good questions and answers stimulate other questions.

Media jargon.   Some of the jargon of journalism has passed into the language, but it has become garbled and misunderstood in the process. It is important when speaking to the media to remember the correct terminology. Everything is 'on the record' unless the opposite is agreed before speaking. One should also remember that:

❏ 'Quote': A journalist will be looking for a quote so that he can write or say that someone said this.

❏ 'Off-the-record': This means simply that it is not to be quoted but is instead background information for the journalist. Too much of this will make an interview worthless unless a journalist has asked for a background briefing 'off-the-record'.

❏ 'Non-attributable': There are times when you want something reported, but might be embarrassed at seeing a name mentioned. A non-attributable comment can be reported but without the source being identified. In newspapers, this might appear as 'a source within', or 'an observer of . . .'.

❏ 'No comment': This leaves the media to draw their own conclusions unless you are able to give a good reason, because a particular topic is *sub judice* for example.

❏ 'Embargo': This restricts publication or broadcast of a news item before a certain time, allowing journalists to prepare and research a complex story. Unnecessary embargoes can irritate or be broken, or in the case of a minor story ensure that this is consigned to oblivion. One should be sensitive to pressures on an embargo; something embargoed to benefit the Sunday newspapers may be used by the Saturday newspapers. A way round this is to release the story by wire or facsimile transmission in time for journalists to work on it, but without an embargo.

The correct terminology for an embargo is to head the press release with:

'EMBARGO: NOT FOR PUBLICATION OR BROADCAST BEFORE [time] HOURS, . . . DAY, DATE'

The concept of the embargoed story is especially appropriate for charities. The most skilled charity workers have known for years the value of announcing the results of research on a Monday. The daily newspapers and their broadcast colleagues will have the weekend to digest and investigate the news under cover of an '00.01 hours, Monday, ...' embargo, thus ensuring far better coverage.

The media are not desperate for another free lunch, if they ever were, although in common with the business community they may be reflecting the increasing pressure of modern times. The opportunity for a long and alcoholic lunch, or a working day on the golf course, is now an extremely rare event. Journalists who are always available for lunch or a reception tend to be the less effective and least reliable. They may linger at the first function they attend during an evening if the alcohol is of the desired quality and quantity.

Freelance journalists in particular, many worth half-a-dozen staff reporters because they need to have stories published, often cannot afford the time or travelling costs involved in attending lightweight and unproductive functions.

These are the main media events:

1. Press conferences: Are ideal for major events, which might include announcing details of an important sponsorship or a major charitable donation, or dealing with a crisis.
2. Press receptions: A cross between lunches and press conferences. Receptions are a good idea if the news story is not strong enough, but sufficient senior people can be fielded for the press to feel that attendance would be useful. They also provide the opportunity for an informal discussion with leading figures in the organisation.
3. Press lunches: Occasional press lunches are useful if linked to an interview or an opportunity to meet senior members of a management team. The ideal is one journalist meeting one or two members of the management team plus the PR person. However, journalists will attend lunches with other journalists present on condition that they know about this arrangement in advance. It enables them to meet senior people of sufficient worth. These lunches establish contact and shouldn't be expected to achieve more than that.

In organising any of these functions, remember to:

❏ Only select and invite those journalists likely to be interested, concentrate on those with a track record in your activity.

❑ It is possible to refine point 2 above, simply by letting journalists know in broad terms what is on offer and why.

❑ Telephone 24 hours before the event to remind the guests and ensure that they are still interested.

❑ Sign all guests in so that there is a record of who attended.

❑ Brief the hosts in advance on who is attending, and any likely issues or interests.

❑ There should be a programme, with a starting time, perhaps with coffee or pre-meal drinks (depending on the time of day), a time for the function itself to start, and a finishing time, which for lunch should be no later than 2.30 pm, so that busy journalists can get away.

❑ Journalists unable to attend should have any material distributed at the function sent to them, both as a courtesy and for information.

❑ Ensure that the timing is convenient for the media. Those working on Sunday newspapers usually do not work on Mondays. Weekly trade and local newspapers appearing on Friday normally go to press on Wednesday – a long and very busy day for the journalists involved.

❑ If at all possible, attempt to avoid clashing with another function of interest to the same journalists. It is not unknown for companies deliberately to compete with their rivals in this way, but it really is counter-productive to do so.

If the event is simply one of making contact, evening functions can be useful. If you are anxious to find your story in the following day's newspapers, late afternoon or early evening functions are too late for all but the most important news. Ideally, time events to take place after 10 am and before 4pm.

INTO THE PRESS ROOM

If you are lucky, the organisers of the sponsored event will have prepared a room for the media, but you might have to take charge of this yourself. Either way, you will need to know what the media expect.

At some sporting events, it is possible to have a room in a

grandstand offering a fine view of proceedings. At a bowls tournament, for example, the press realise that they often have to get out and watch from the sidelines.

The essentials of a good press room are:

1. Accessibility: The press will want to interview players; any press room must not present an obstacle course to a journalist in a hurry.
2. Adequate accommodation: Nothing will spoil the event more than journalists fighting over desks and chairs.
3. Suitable facilities: Telephones, fax machines, photocopiers and modems for computer data links are all necessities for journalists attempting to get their reports to their newspapers quickly. You can also ensure that there is an adequate supply of tea and coffee. Alcoholic drink is not necessary, and the best wouldn't expect it.
4. Sensitive staffing: Having staff on hand to sort out any problems, collate and distribute results, and ensure that everything works smoothly, will make the operation more efficient. Although one won't need senior people, those chosen will need skill and tact, and the ability to cope with a long day.

ON THE AIR

Broadcast coverage of sponsored events is so important that it is usual for many sponsorship agreements to offer two levels of funding. The higher level will apply if broadcast coverage is achieved. It is also feasible to confine sponsorship only to those events or activities that will be broadcast.

Major sporting events can always be guaranteed broadcast coverage. The organisers will be collecting a considerable fee from the broadcasters in addition to ticket sales and sponsorship.

The problems arise with those activities that are marginal. Ideally the organisers, but often the sponsors, may need to negotiate directly with the broadcasters. Timing of events, and even their location, might need to be adjusted to suit the broadcasting schedules. More complicated is the fact that the independent television companies will usually only be able to offer transmissions within their own region. It is much harder to ensure national coverage on independent television.

Negotiating with broadcasters.

The BBC is much easier in this respect, but the heavy load of programming and the cost of outside broadcasts can be additional obstacles. Do not turn down the chance of the event being televised on BBC 2 – the followers of a particular sport can be guaranteed to do just that. It is certainly more effective than being confined to a single ITV region.

Broadcasters in the UK accept that sponsors merit two mentions during a full length broadcast, although this does not apply if it is a brief soundbite for a news bulletin or sports roundup. The rules are fairly standard throughout Europe and reflect the approach of the European Broadcasting Union.

Broadcasting rules.

The rules over publicising your sponsorship or your company and its brands at the location will be limited. In planning the positioning of cameras, the director will ensure that every time the camera pans across the pitch, the picture is not dominated by mentions of the sponsor. At one boxing match, the sponsor was told to remove a large banner over the ring, or no broadcast. The independent television companies appear to be stricter than the BBC. This surprises many but may be due to a culture more accustomed to screening advertisements, and which is anxious to ensure that event sponsorship is not a low cost alternative to television advertising or programme sponsorship.

CHECKLIST

- Ensure that your company's press office and/or PR consultants are aware of your sponsorship ambitions and any significant charitable donations before serious negotiations start.
- In any sponsorship or charitable activity, agree with the organisers that any communications about your company's involvement be cleared through your press office or PR consultancy.
- Let the organisers know what you are doing, so that they can see your press releases about the sponsorship before these are issued.
- Assess just how effective the media relations support of the sponsored event will be, so that you can decide whether you need to provide additional resources.
- Consider media training for your colleagues and directors who may be expected to speak on the company's behalf about sponsorship or charitable donations.
- Don't waste the time of journalists by inviting them to press conferences that have little real point.
- Ensure that media releases are short and factual – hard facts, not hype, will ensure media coverage.

Chapter 9

Assessing the Results

There are those who believe that it is difficult to quantify the benefits of sponsorship, and impossible to assess the benefits to the company of charitable donations. This is true if sponsorship is conducted by whim, or charitable donations were no more than token gestures spreading the available largesse widely, but never seeming generous or involved. Good sponsorship can be chosen by instinct, but how do you know that it is good?

Those sponsorships that suit the personal tastes of a senior member of the board can be disregarded. So can those that the chairman or chief executive has been forced into accepting to satisfy their peer group. Politicians, at all levels, seem to be past masters at persuading chairmen and chief executives to support this or that cause. Such pressures have been accepted willingly in the hope of a mention in an honours list! Perhaps that would be one means of assessing the results.

The personal tastes of the senior management team cannot be overlooked completely when judging whether a sponsorship or a charitable donations policy has been successful. It is important to consider what is being judged, by whom, and why.

MONITORING SPONSORSHIP

Sponsorship has to justify itself. There will be many critics waiting to pounce if they scent failure. This is more serious than with many other activities. Those who would have preferred their own favourite event or activity to be sponsored will be ready to show how right they were. The advertising agency will be keen to demonstrate how much more could have been achieved if the same money had been devoted to increased advertising. Anything as high profile as sponsorship will always be a target for the 'I told you so' brigade and for those who feel that the money could have been put to so much better use by themselves.

Using tracking research.

Research showing that the sponsorship was the right choice in the beginning cannot stand on its own for too long. It will need to be supported by tracking research, recording changes in perceptions or awareness, and by subjective and objective assessments by your colleagues:

❏ At the beginning, research showing how aware the target audience is of your company or its products should be done.

❏ At intervals, the awareness of this audience and its attitudes to the organisation and to its sponsorship should also be researched. Regular opinion tracking is always useful and may allow some adjustments to the programme and to any supporting promotional activity.

❏ Media coverage should be monitored including mentions of the sponsorship.

❏ Feedback from those hosting guests should be monitored. Managers or representatives should advise you of any new customers or new business arising from the sponsorship.

❏ If customers have the opportunity to obtain free or discounted tickets to attend an event, the number taking advantage of this should be recorded.

The use of sponsorship to raise a company's profile and improve its image is a major reason for undertaking the exercise in the first place. Figure 2.1 showed a favourability/familiarity profile for a number of companies, undertaken by Market and Opinion Research International (MORI).

One note of caution in considering such research is that not all audiences will respond in the same way. The average consumer can feel well-disposed towards familiar companies, but other audiences are far more cynical as Figure 2.2 shows. Investment analysts and journalists will be more cynical and critical of any company they know really well. This is because they will be aware of major problems or weaknesses not immediately apparent to those with a more superficial understanding of the company.

Tracking research and assessing media coverage will show that considered and targeted sponsorship can be quantified as can any other business activity. This is also possible with charitable donations.

The strengths and weaknesses of the different methods of monitoring vary, as one might expect.

RESEARCH

If not handled properly and professionally, research can reflect the prejudices of the individual who has commissioned it. But it remains the single most effective method of assessing the situation. It is also one of the more expensive.

Good objective research needs to be conducted externally. Specialists will appreciate that the phrasing of the questions can influence the answers. Measuring the effectiveness of a particular sponsorship programme should begin with research into the target audience before the campaign starts. Research should also be carried out during the sponsorship if it lasts more than a year, and repeated when it has finished. Only in this way can effectiveness be measured on a programmed basis.

External research.

Qualitative research is based on interviews and identifies specific responses or reactions, sometimes attributing these to individuals. Research has to be confined to a limited audience to be manageable, for example, investment analysts interested in a particular sector of industry, or politicians interested in a particular policy area. Research can use groups or panels and may be conducted by a psychologist. This technique is often used when new products or new advertising campaigns are being evaluated.

Qualitative research.

Quantitative research poses questions to a larger number of people, but seldom looks for more than a 'yes' or 'no' answer. The best examples of such research are the opinion polls conducted to assess the electoral preferences of the population. A thousand or so people are asked for their political allegiances and whether certain politicians are good or bad at their particular role. In industry, such research is often conducted into product preferences.

Quantitative research.

For sponsorships, quantitative research is more suitable than qualitative as they are designed to raise the image of a company or brand with a mass audience.

Researchers will need a brief to formulate a draft questionnaire and estimate the costs and the timescale. Experienced researchers will advise on suitable times of the year, month, week, or even the day for conducting research to catch the ideal audience.

Bought-in research. Major research companies have regular research programmes of their own, and anyone interested in the sector can subscribe to the results. This is much cheaper than going it alone, and you can compare your own organisation with your rivals more easily. Difficulties include being unable to exert much influence on the questions and the audience on which the research is being conducted. It is often not possible to use the results in publicity as these are copyright and belong to the research company. However, if such omnibus research projects are available, subscribing to them is an inexpensive way of providing information. It is a starting point from which to plan other specific commissioned research. Ignoring omnibus research could mean re-inventing the wheel, and at great cost.

There are regular research programmes covering a variety of industries. Examples include those conducted by MORI into the opinions of business finance and personal finance journalists. The research looks at their views on specific companies, their management, products, and not least their media relations.

Research panels. Research using small groups of people or panels can be useful, especially in tracking trends, but can be difficult to organise and retain the interest and enthusiasm of those involved. A problem that arises particularly when validating marketing campaigns and television advertising is that the results provided are those that the panel members believe the commissioner wants.

The group of people where qualitative research can be useful will be your company's own employees. This is one means of discovering how they feel about sponsorship and charitable donations. If they have been involved, especially in fund-raising events for a charitable appeal, has this changed their attitude towards the company? Much will depend on the prevailing atmosphere within the company. If it is good, qualitative research could be worthwhile, otherwise, frank opinions might be difficult to obtain rendering the research valueless.

It is never good enough to conduct research simply by sending a questionnaire. The response will be patchy and mainly confined to those critical of whatever is being provided.

MONITORING PRESS AND BROADCAST COVERAGE

Sponsorship is meant to increase the number of media mentions obtained by the sponsor. Whereas the prime requirement in most public relations activity is to obtain a 'good press', in the case of sponsorship most media comment will be neutral unless the sponsor and the organisers become embroiled in some controversy.

One way of assessing whether media coverage is satisfactory is to retain a good press cuttings agency. Another is to use a company to monitor broadcasts, provide transcripts whenever the sponsor is mentioned, and provide video tapes of television coverage.

Press cuttings agencies.

No press cuttings agency is better than 70 per cent effective. References will be missed and as some are better in dealing with one type of publication than another it is worth using two agencies. Some broadcast monitoring services are faster than others, but the slower ones are usually larger. These can provide complete nationwide coverage of local radio and regional television as well as national broadcasts.

You cannot scan every newspaper or magazine yourself. They would be expensive even though most PR functions buy the main national and the relevant regional newspapers and magazines. The more mentions in the media, the more likely that the press cuttings agencies and broadcast monitors will recall that your company is a client.

Cuttings agencies and broadcast monitors work in different ways, and charge differently as well. Cuttings agencies automatically cut, despatch and charge for everything they find. The broadcast monitors offer a transcript or tape to the client, which can be refused before it is transcribed and despatched.

Broadcast monitors.

These differences reflect the different costs of the two types of business. Cuttings are relatively inexpensive, transcripts and tapes are more costly. Although individual cuttings might cost more than the newspaper from which they have been cut, this is still less expensive than buying and attempting to read everything.

The means of assessing the value of these services are:

1. Measure the number of cuttings and the relevance of the newspapers. The same can be done with broadcast mentions.

2. Measure the length of each cutting, or transcript, so that this can be translated into column inches or centimetres, or minutes or hours of air time.

3. Evaluate the coverage by relating the space or time to advertising rates. This will only be a rough guide because it cannot provide a cost that reflects the position on the page or the different value of different pages in terms of advertising rate. Neither can it account for the fact that editorial is read or listened to when advertising would be ignored. However, as the BBC does not carry advertising any rate comparison becomes of doubtful value. Nevertheless, such comparisons can be highly influential with senior management.

4. Assess whether the coverage is favourable or unfavourable to the organisation and its objectives. Normally, it will be neutral, but sponsors can be praised for making a particular event possible, or more widely available. They can also be criticised if arrangements are poor, blatantly commercial, or if the sponsor and organiser fall out.

JUDGING BY RESULTS

Any assessment by results should be on business gained, but this is difficult to quantify in sponsorship. Targets can be set for improved familiarity and favourability and when research shows these have been achieved, the programme can be declared a success. These targets should be set realistically after earlier research shows the existing position.

Evidence from corporate hospitality.

The corporate hospitality element can be used to see whether existing business connections are maintained, or new and successful connections established. This can be assessed by asking the company officials acting as hosts whether those on their guest lists are still doing business with the company, or have started doing so. If the guests are sufficiently valuable, the manager or sales representative dealing with them should be able to assess the business gained.

The attitude of local people or politicians towards the company will provide an indication of the success of a social sponsorship project.

CHARITABLE DONATIONS

Companies dispensing charitable donations widely will find that they have little real contact with the charities themselves. Typically, a request is received, processed, and either a polite refusal is sent or a cheque.

Those who are more selective and provide large individual donations will only do so after detailed consideration. The company will often be proactive by seeking those charities whose objectives match its own.

Social sponsorship can be assessed using the parameters applied to other forms of sponsorship, even though you might be inclined to be a little less exacting in your assessments, given the hybrid nature of the enterprise.

In the case of donations, the measurement of results will be more difficult. Favourable media coverage when large cheques are handed over, perhaps? You can assess the impact that you are making with the charity and its supporters, and whether this has any substantial value.

You must appreciate, and ensure that your management appreciates, that a charitable donation is not always the same as sponsorship. You can overlap with social sponsorship and involvement in community projects, but many donations will go largely unnoticed and unsung, which is perhaps what it is all about.

Bibliography and Further Information

BIBLIOGRAPHY

Charity Forum News, 54 Church Street, Tisbury, Salisbury, Wilts, SP3 6NH Tel: 0747 870490

The Directory of Social Change, Radius Works, Back Lane, London NW3 1HL Tel: 071-435 8171

Hollis Sponsorship & Donations Yearbook, Hollis Directories, Contact House, Sunbury-on-Thames, Middx, TW16 5HG Tel: 0932 784781

Sponsorship News, PO Box 66, Wokingham, Berks, RG11 4RQ Tel: 0734 772770

Sponsorship Yearbook, Hobsons Publishing plc, Bateman Street, Cambridge, CB2 1LZ Tel: 0223 354551

ADDRESSES

Arts Council of Great Britain, 14 Great Peter Street, London SW1P 3NQ Tel: 071-333 0100

Association for Business Sponsorship of the Arts, ABSA, Nutmeg House, 60 Gainsford Street, London SE1 2NY Tel: 071-378 8143

European Committee for Business Arts and Culture, CREC, Nutmeg House, 60 Gainsford Street, London SE1 2NY Tel: 071-378 8143

Institute of Sports Sponsorship, Francis House, Francis Street, London SW1P 1DE Tel: 071-828 8771

The Sponsorship Advisory Service, c/o The Sports Council, 16 Upper Woburn Place, London WC1H 0QP Tel: 071-388 1277

The Sponsorship Advisory Service for Scotland, c/o The Scottish Sports Council, Caledonian House, South Gyle, Edinburgh, EH12 9DQ Tel: 031-317 7200

The Sponsorship Association, 16 Partridge Close, Chesham, Bucks, HP5 3LH Tel: 0494 775710

European Sponsorship Consultants Association, ESCA, 16 Partridge Close, Chesham, Bucks, HP5 3LH Tel: 0494 791760

Business in the Community, 8 Stratton Street, London W1X 5FD Tel: 071-629 1600

The Council for Industry and Higher Education, 100 Park Village East, London NW1 3SR Tel: 071-387 2171

National Council for Voluntary Organisations, 26 Bedford Square, London WC1B 3HU Tel: 071-636 4066

Scottish Council for Voluntary Organisations, 18/19 Claremont Crescent, Edinburgh EH7 4QD Tel: 031-556 3882

Index